A Bird is Not a Stone

An anthology of contemporary Palestinian poetry

**FREIGHT
BOOKS**

First published in the UK June 2014
By Freight Books
49-53 Virginia Street
Glasgow, G1 1TS
www.freightbooks.co.uk

A CIP catalogue reference for this book is available from the British
Library.

ISBN 978-1-908754-56-1

Typeset by Freight in Adobe Caslon Pro and Myriad Arabic
Printed and bound by Bell and Bain, Glasgow

the publisher acknowledges investment from
Creative Scotland toward the publication of this book

Contents

Maya Abu Al-Hayyat

Foreword
Maya Abu Al-Hayyat

Yes, he wants to say, translating poetry won't be easy.
How can it, if the poem itself is merely the translation
of feelings so subtle that you barely experience,
or so strong that you can hardly contain them?

Makarand Paranjape- A modern Indian poet

نكتب الشعر، لأننا لا نستطيع أن نكتب شيئًا آخر، نكتبه لأنه الترجمة الوحيدة لما نريد أن
نقول. إنها اللغة الوحيدة التي نعرف، لغة لا ترجمة حرفية لها ولا تأويل واحد لفعلها. فهل
يمكن ترجمة الشعر؟ هذا السؤال القديم الجديد الذي لم يعد يعني أحدا، يخطر ببالي الآن
وأنا أفكر بأهمية ترجمة مختارات من الشعر الفلسطيني إلى لغة أخرى، أهمية ترجمة القول
الإنساني واللحظة الشعرية التي لا يمكن أن تتشابه لاختلاف ظروف الكتابة. الكتابة التي لا
يمكن أن تنفصل عن الظرف المكاني والزماني والسياسي للكاتب الذي يحاول (بشكل فردي) رصد
لحظته الخاصة ضمن وجوده الإنساني العام.
ربما من الأفضل الأسحاب من العام ودفع السؤال للشخصنة وأنا أفكر بأن هناك من سيقرأ
شعري الذي يبدو محليا بمفرداته وظرف حدوثه. هذا القارئ، الكاتب الثاني للنص، كيف سيقرأ
نص شاعرة من فلسطين تخوض حروبها اليومية كإمرأة وأم وفلسطينية وشاعرة تفكر باللغة
والمجاز وتجاوز ما قيل ليس فقط محليا بل عالميا إيضا.
الشعر الذي اعتبر على مدى سنوات مضت مقولة الفلسطيني الإنسانية التي يدافع بها عما يراد
إلصاقه به من صور، وهو يحاول تحديد هويته كل مرة من خلاله ليفهم ويترجم ما يسمعه
ويراه ويحركه بلغة مدهشة وموازية تصل إلى العالم.
وأجد من المناسب في الحديث عن أهمية ترجمة الشعر الفلسطيني استعراض التغييرات التي
طرأت على الشعر الفلسطيني الحديث على مدى الأعوام السابقة.

Palestinian poetry has reflected the political, geographic, and human changes that Palestine and the Arab world have been through since the first World War, including the Nakba, the 1967 war and defeat, the first uprising (Intifada), Oslo, and everything that followed.

Poetry has reflected these changes across theme, form, audience, inner voice, metaphor and technical structure.

It may be said that modern poetry has formed in the era of image, images that are available in all means of communication, images made available by official and oppressive regimes that use them to obstruct speech and control thoughts.

We recall the period of the first Intifada when Israel prohibited Palestinians from raising their flag, singing their national anthem or keeping pictures of PLO fighters or Abu Ammar, and when curricula were restricted and all autonomist actions were monitored and prohibited within Palestinian borders. In that period, mythical, metaphoric and figurative language was the essential tool in modern poetry, as illustrated in the poems of Mahmoud Darwish, Samih Al-Qasim, and Fadwa Tuqan, which all sing for one female: Palestine. All girls and all love stories, all sacrifices and all mothers are, at the end of the poem, transformed into the homeland, the land, or the home.

Concepts changed after Oslo, and literature that had once glorified the resistance became 'old fashioned'. There was both new openness and new alienation in the cultural sphere. This clash was brought about by the convergence of the idea and the actuality of the homeland: between those returning and the residents, between the dream and the truth – the dream of access to the homeland and the reality that emerged after Oslo.

Poetry was hit by a similar state of confusion. It relied on experimentation in an attempt to come up with a new form and a new language, but it remained caught between symbolism and metaphor. This has been the case with the 1990s generation of poets, who identified themselves as young poets and who were perhaps unlucky to emerge in this time of transition, in this middle time. That is to say, they were not totally free, nor were they completely classical; their poems relied heavily on linguistic spectacle, the manipulation of pronouns and form.

We notice that most of the poetry particular to this generation was very vague. They used words like mirrors, shadows, absence, presence, words that revealed the process of discovery and transformation from one state to another. They dealt with viewing things in a different way, exactly parallel to the political situation at that period.

After the second Intifada, which put Palestinians in a no war/no peace situation and where the world turned out to be a world of movies controlled by a million satellite stations, with internet and social media that offered everyone a platform to broadcast their own particular views; After the dissolution of most Arab regimes and the transformation of communities from oppression, to societies where anything can be said of them at any time, reference points for identifying poetry disappeared. No one can know what poetry is or should be, or who is a poet.

Even contemporary critics avoid exploring such ideas; because when you acknowledge this multifarious space of transmitting and receiving, you must acknowledge that no one can evaluate the experience of the other as rendered in text (such as poetry), whether it subsists or vanishes in time.

Is there any room for metaphors now?

I have always maintained that no metaphoric language is capable of capturing the face of a child covered with ash, raided by his own government's planes in Syria, or another's in Lebanon or Gaza without cause or meaning; or at least without a cause that the mind can comprehend.

Metaphors cannot keep pace with the tremendous power of images to control us, the power to which we are daily exposed in the modern world. As a result of technological development, the media is not so far from an everyday control of our emotions and beliefs. And so you cannot confirm anything absolutely by yourself when surrounded by this surfeit of images and influence. If you are controlled by these outside images than logically you cannot believe anything.

All this reflects to a great extent on poetry, not only in Palestine but in the entire world. Poems are full of doubt, undermining solid logic, highlighting absurdity beyond truth, and focusing on the untruthfulness of absolute facts.

إذا هل أصبحنا نتكلم لغة واحدة الآن يمكن ترجمتها إلى كل اللغات فتعطي نفس المفهوم.
أحب أن أؤمن بذلك.

Liz Lochhead

Foreword

Liz Lochhead

July 2012. We're staying for a few nights as guests in Aida Camp in Bethlehem. This 'temporary' Refugee Camp of six hundred and fifty or so families, four thousand people, is, it strikes me, exactly as old as me – having been established under a terrified flurry of canvas tents in 1948 as the grandparents and parents of the present generation either fled for their lives or were – at best – forcibly displaced from their homes and villages as the State of Israel was created. Now it is a permanent, overcrowded, ramshackle, ad-hoc, self-build sink-housing-scheme lookalike, albeit with brave wee creative and personal decorative motifs here and there (a mural, a fancy finial). Ever vertically expanding to ac-commodate its ever-expanding population, it's cramped into far, far too small an area, hemmed in on one side by a lavish new brutalist four-star tourist hotel complex, on others by the observation towers of the Israeli Defence Force, built right into the camp's boundary walls.

Bored young Israeli conscripts with very big guns look down on the street life just a few feet below them. Just out-of-school weans playing with their pet cats, climbing in and out of skips and rubble; somebody running home at dinnertime with a tower of pitta-bread sandwiches hot and fragrant from the falafel shop; young men hunkered and smok-ing, laughing and sharing banter with the wee crowds of girls passing in their bright jeans and skimpy, tight t-shirts, in the hijab headscarf or without it, who give back as good as they get.

All everyone wants us to do is 'tell the world we are not terrorists.'

No shower this morning, none for the last four days, just another rub-down with baby wipes, no unnecessary flushing of toilets. The water, stored in the tanks on the roofs, has just about run out again. Most inhabitants just shrug. Ach, they'll probably turn it on again in a day or two, they do so for a few days every three weeks or so, the trouble is you never know when…

We're going on to East Jerusalem to stay. None of our Aida Camp hosts can come there too, though it's just over five miles away. Their identity papers confine them to the West Bank. They try and explain to me about the Green Line, the different classes of travel papers …

The petty, daily harassments the Palestinians have to endure are impossible to imagine unless you witness them first hand. This is not to speak of the Wall, the settlements, the huge historical injustice of the Nakba, Palestine's catastrophe of 1948.

It's Apartheid. The State of Israel denies human rights to Palestinians. Denies that they are human beings at all.

There're the 'wee things', like the contempt and arrogance of the soldier demanding the passports at Qalandia Checkpoint… Then there is the heart-breaking testimony of the man in the tent in the desert with his thin sheep and scrawny goats among the burning, blasted stones, tares and thistles of the Jordan Valley. He has endured two house demolitions, has rebuilt and resisted but, finally broken, is giving up and moving to the ghetto of the nearby 'city' because the Israelis disrupt the service of the school bus every other day, and he just can't bear to see his children deprived of an education…

We witness first hand the terror of the tear gas and the rubber bullets (no 'skunk water' and only one live round today, thank goodness) of the IDF at the weekly Friday post-prayers peaceful demonstration against the Wall in the olive-growing village of Ni'lin.

We are a little ad-hoc group of mostly young poets and songwriters (William Letford – Billy – is the nearest to my age, though more than a quarter-of-a-century my junior. Most are fifteen years younger than him.) There's a Gael, a Scot or two, a couple of young Englishman, one a recently graduated film-maker who is documenting our experiences.

When we go to The House of Poetry in Ramallah to which Henry Bell (one of the editors of this book, arguably its prime mover and maker) has managed, in between his Glasgow University finals, to negotiate a visit from our group, we can't but notice on the facade the bullet-holes in the lintels of the door, the ugly silhouette of two settlements on the brow of the hill opposite.

How does poetry deal with such a reality? What else but poetry has the beauty, truth and courage to try.

Amongst the people we met was a group of the principal Palestinian poets in the House of Poetry in Ramallah. Talking with them (with the aid of a completely fluent, colloquial and sparky translator, they didn't speak English) we quickly had to confront just how profoundly ignorant we were of Palestinian poetry – beyond the brilliant Darwish, one of the few to have been translated widely into English.

This was particularly embarrassing as the poet Murad Sudani, the distinguished director of The House of Poetry, talked so fondly and eruditely about Edwin Morgan…

These poets told us how when they were – rarely – translated into English it was always by academics and generally to be quoted as part of polemical, theoretical or literary essays and in obscure publications. They were made into far less than poems, or were sometimes effectively censored by the omission of some of their content.

At best, it wasn't the thing, it was about the thing …

They stressed the obvious – that poetry needs to be translated by poets, made into new poems; were excited by the prospect of an anthology in which, for a start, Palestinian poets themselves chose which poems of theirs would be translated.

And so, working with the House of Poetry, The General Union of Palestinian Writers, The Scottish Poetry Library, and Freight Books, greatly helped by both Robyn Marsack and, especially, by Sarah Irving -the other originator and editor- and the Arabic department at the University of Edinburgh, this book has come into being. You hold in your hand, or are accessing online, a bi-lingual, made-in-Scotland anthology of contemporary Palestinian poetry in English, Scots, Scots-English, Gaelic and Shetlandic.

Sarah and a volunteer army of translators worked with the Palestinian poets for several months and produced the first 'bridge translations.' Many from among the very most distinguished poets of this country gave freely of their time and talent to make versions of many, many more poems than we could ever fit into this volume.

Surely translating poetry is impossible? Of course.

If, as John Glenday said recently, 'Everything we write is translation… First of all I translate an initial impetus/feeling/notion into words.' Nevertheless we must accept it is impossible as a poet to translate our reader (As simple a thing as the word 'horse', for instance, does not, cannot have the bred-in-the-bone symbolic meaning for us as it does for the Arabic poet). But still, something deep will always communicate. Only poetry has the absolute ability to transcend borders and cultures, connect human beings.

طارق الكرمي

أسطورةٌ مُطهَّمَةٌ

لا حِصانَ ريتشاردَ..لا البيقوريةَ مركبُ الإسكندرِ
لا أحصِنةَ روما الفاتحةِ أرضَ الجنِّ
لا حِصانَ طروادةَ ظلَّ
كلُّ أحصنةِ العالمِ لمْ تعُدْ المُطَهّمةَ
كلُّها كبتْ تكبو أو
قَضَتْ بالرّصاصةِ الرّحيمةِ
كُلُّها
إلاّ الذي ابتاعهُ أبي لي
حِصاني و
إنْ كانَ مِنْ خشبْ

فَقْرٌ

كلُّ الفياغرا
لنْ تجعلَ الوضعَ اللإقتصادي
مُنتصِباًيَقِفُ.

Tareq al-Karmy
Bridge translations by Sandra Ernst

The Legend of Mythic, Proud Perfection

Not Richard's – not your "Lionheart"'s – horse, no
Nor Great Alexander's steed Bucephalus, no
Not Roman horses thundering home their demonic mastery,
Not the legendary, immortal, Trojan horse,
No, there's never been a horse on all the earth but –
failing to attain absolute perfection of nobility –
has, in the end, had to be put down
by merciful bullets. Not one
except
this, the one my father bought me,
my horse,
although it's only wee and made of wood.

Liz Lochhead

Poverty

All the Viagra in the world
won't
make the economy
stand up.

Liz Lochhead

عنِ الطِّفلةِ

أرأيتَ كيفَ قنصَ الجُنديُّ الطِّفلةَ (عندَ نهدِها الأيسرِ الذي لمْ ينتأ بعدُ)..كانتْ (ما تزالُ) تموتُ برهافةِ أوراقِ الخسِّ...لكنَّ الطِّفلةَ هذي هي أختي (فرضاً)..إبنةُ مَنْ لمْ يُنجِبْها البتَّة..مشروعُ «مريمَ» ما..عقيلتي التي لمْ أتزوّجْها قطُّ..أخيراً هي أمّي المؤجِّلةُ أبداً

حينَ الحنينُ

على قبورِ إخوتي
على الأرضِ
عليكِ
على نفسي
على الطِّفلِ
كقوسِ قزحٍ أنحني

*ليلاً \ شتاءُ طورِ كرمِ

About the Wee Girl

Man, you saw how the soldier shot the wee girl
straight through what
would have become her left breast?
She continues to die, over and over, like a
perpetual withering of young green leaves.
I am beholden to her, my sister,
my daughter who will never give birth,
my wife I can never marry,
my Maryam, my sacred one,
my mother forever.

Liz Lochhead

An Epoch of Remembering

Over the graves of my brothers
over the earth
over you my love
over myself
over the child
I bend like a rainbow

Liz Lochhead

ليستْ إلاّ أنهاراً

مِنْ أينَ يَنْبُعُ أيُّ شارعٍ
أينَ يَصبُّ وأيَّ مُرتوىً سيمضي
ليسَ يَهمُّ اسمُ الشّارعِ
ليسَ يَهمُّ أيّةَ مدينةٍ يفتضُّ أو
أيَّ قُرىً يَتَغلْغلُ
مادامتِ النّاسُ..العرباتُ و
السّياراتُ..
إلخ..
ستبقى أبداً أسماكَ الشّارعْ

*صباحاً \ طور كرم

الهندسةُ

حينما تفتحينَ ساقيكِ مثلَ فِرجارٍ
على مصراعي الفِرجارِ
في اللّحظةِ المدارِ حينَ ندحو بعضَنا
فهل ستفعلينَ
إلاّ هندسةً أجهلُها (مثلَ زواياً للدّائرة)
سترتسمينَ للأرض
مُثلّثَ دائرةِ الأرضْ...

*صباحاً \ طور كرم

Not only Rivers

Not only rivers have a source.
  Paths trickle from single dwellings till,
  fed by tracks from villages, they go
  through towns and cities. Swelled
  by tributary streets till they end
  in mighty ports and seaside resorts.
  Roads die when peoples' hopes, fears,
  wishes, traffic, no longer flow through them,
  unlike rivers which are not made by fishes.

Alasdair Gray

The Engineering

O my woman, when you
open your legs like a drafting-compass,
a wide open compass,
in that orbital moment when we stretch each other in sex
tell me, is it going to happen for you?
It is only engineering I am ignorant of (like
the impossible angles of a circle).
You are about to make a graphic image of the whole world,
the triangle and the circle of the earth.

Liz Lochhead

قميصُ نومِر فتاتي.

قميصُ نومكِ الذي كالماءِ يرقُّ عليكِ
قميصُكِ هذا الذي يشِفُّ حتى ملمسِ الهواءِ
عليهِ رَسمُ دُبّيْ باندا
لماذا كلَّ صباحٍ حينَ أُصَبِّحكِ خيراً
يتثاءبُ دُبّا الباندا في قميصِكِ
يقفزانِ مِنْ قميصِكِ و
يهجُمانِ عليَّ يُداعباني
هُما دُبّاكِ الباندا
*صباحاً \ طور كرم

اللقاءُ بالأرضِ

في بلادي حيثُ بلادي
لِمَ يسقطُ القتيلُ على وجهِهِ
فاتحاً ذراعيهِ
أهوَ يسقطُ على وجهِهِ لأنُه يسقطُ على وجهِهِ وحسبُ
أهوَ الذي حينَ يسقطُ على وجهِهِ
فاتحاً ذراعيهِ

إلا ليحضُنَ الأرضَ..

*مساءً \ طور كرم

The Sleeping Shirt of my Girl

The sleeping shirt wrapped around you like water –
The shirt so thin you can feel the wind –
On it are two pandas.

And so… in the morning when I say 'Good morning'
Your two pandas yawn on your sleeping shirt,
Your two pandas jump from your shirt to me,
They tease me, play with me –
Your two panda bears!

Ron Butlin

Meeting With The Ground

In the country where my country is,
Whoever's killed does not fall on his face
Opening his arms,
Does he fall on his face simply because
He falls on his face – end of story?

Or does he fall on his face
Opening his arms
Wide – to embrace the whole earth?

Ron Butlin

زهيـر أبو شـايب

شهيـد

وجَدوه أخضرَ كالضياءِ
وعندما رفعوا يدَه
وجدوا السنابلَ أفئدة
ويُقالُ : زقزقت السنابلُ تحتَ كمِّه
ويُقالُ : أحضَرت الطيورُ دماءَه لبناتِ عمِّه
ويُقالُ : سوفَ يعودُ
في شجَرِ البراكينِ الخفيِّ
وسوفَ يملأُ صدرَ أمِّه
لكنّهم وجدوه أخضرَ كالضياءِ
وكفّنوه بزرِّ وردة
فرشوا لبسمتِه السماءَ
وكانت الشمسُ المِخدّة

Zuhair Abu Shaib
Bridge translations by Zoe Dexter

Martyr

When they found him
he had become an emerald flame;
and when they lifted his arms they found
sheaves of wheat where a heart should be;
and they say those sheaves were whispering
beneath his shirt; and they say the wild birds
ferried his blood to his family, drop by drop;
and they say he will come back, suspended
in the hidden tree at the burning heart of volcanoes
and that his mother will fold him in her arms.
But when they found him he was an emerald flame,
so they stitched together rose petals for a shroud
and smoothed out the sky to keep him warm
and for a pillow, they lifted down the sun
and laid it beneath his head.

John Glenday

شهــيـد

وجَدوه أخضَرَ كالضياءِ
وعندما رفعوا يَدَه
وجدوا السنابلَ أفئدة
ويُقالُ : زقزقت السنابلُ تحتَ كمِّه
ويُقالُ : أحضَرَت الطيورُ دماءَه لبناتِ عمِّه
ويُقالُ : سوفَ يعودُ
في شجَرِ البراكينِ الخفيِّ
وسوفَ يملأُ صدرَ أمِّه
لكنّهم وجدوه أخضَرَ كالضياءِ
وكفَّنوه بزرِّ وردة
فرشوا لبسمتِه السماءَ
وكانت الشمسُ المِخدّة

martair

fhuair iad a luisneachadh gorm
is 'n uair a thog iad a làmh
fhuair iad sguaban chridhe
agus theirte: rinn na sguaban ceilearaich fo mhuilcheann
agus theirte: thug na h-eòin fhuil d' a chàirdean
agus theirte: tillidh e
ann an craobh fhalaichte bholcànan
is lìonaidh e broilleach a mhàthair
ach fhuair iad e luisneachadh gorm
agus phaisge iad ann 'n guc ròis e
agus sgaoil iad an speur dha ghàire
's bha ghrian na cluasag dha

Aonghas MacNeacail

Zuhair Abu Shaib

صلاةُ استسقاء

قِفي يا روابي
قِفي كي تمرَّ السحابةُ
من بين أضلاعِنا خِلسةً
ويرى الغيثُ صورتَه في الترابِ
قِفي كي نطيّرَ أرواحَنا بهدوءٍ قليلٍ
ونركضَ في إثرِها
إلى سِدرة المنتهى

على حزنها انتظرتْنا البيوتُ ،
هناكَ على طرَفِ الأرضِ ،
كالأمّهاتِ ،
وكنّا نطيّرُ أرواحَنا غرِبَ كلَّ غرابٍ
ونركضُ في إثرِها
إلى سِدرة المنتهى
وكنّا سنبكي ، ولكنّنا ..
.. نسينا .

13

Rain Prayer

Rise up, hills!
Rise up that the clouds might steal through our chests
and for the rain to see its image in the soil

Rise up that we may let our souls take off
like kites, calm in the sky,
and run after them
until we reach the Sidrat al-Muntaha

The houses waited for us, sadly, like mothers
there on the edge of the land
as we flew our kite-souls West of any raven
into the far unknown, and we followed
until we reached the Sidrat al-Muntaha

We would have cried
but we forgot

Ellen McAteer

ذئبٌ مقطَّر

لم تَزَلْ رائحتي فيَّ وشيطاني معي
أفتحُ العتمةَ كالبابِ ،
وأُرمي جسدي منها ،
وأمشي في الأساطيرِ وراءَ امرأةٍ
تعرفُني أكثرَ متِّي
هذه رائحتي الأُولى ،
ولكن شَيْبُ مَن هذا الّذي يملأُ رأسي ؟!
هذه رائحتي
يعرفُها الذئبُ الّذي قطَّرتُه في الليلِ
والريحُ الّتي تشبهُ يأسي

لم تُضِئْني امرأةٌ بَعدُ
ولم تَّبنِ ليَ الطيْرُ من الريش
سماءً بجناحيْنِ
لكي أعرفَ نفسي

Wolf-Scent

My scent hasn't left me, and my demon still follows me...
I open the darkness like a door
And shove my body through it
And I walk, in a fable, behind a woman
Who knows me better than I do myself
This is my first scent
But whose white hair now covers my head?
This is my scent
The wolf, which I sent into the night, knows the wind
Which is the image of my abandoned hope
No woman has shone upon me yet
And no bird has built from her feathers
A heaven with two wings
Where I will know myself.

Henry King

جهة خامسة

خلفَ هذا الصقيع
فُرصةٌ من دمٍ دافٍ كالصلاةِ
ونجمٌ رضيع
طائرُ الضَّوْءِ مختبئٌ خلفَ رائحةِ الجُرحِ
لا ريشُه يابسٌ في مضيقٍ الفضاءِ
ولا الريحُ في دمِه يابسة
كامنٌ في حواشي الفصولِ
يرتّبُ جثّتَه الفارسة
كامنٌ خلفَ هذا الصقيع
يحشدُ الضوْءَ والزقزقاتِ الأميرةَ
والعطرَ والأجنحة
ليعودَ الربيع
للشرايينِ، للخضرةِ العابسة
جهةً خامسة

A Fifth Direction

beneath the frost there is the possibility
of warm blood   like a prayer

a bird made of light   an infant star
secreted behind festering wounds

his feathers are not shrivelled
in the valley of nothingness

nor is the wind in his blood
arid or encrusted

hidden in the footnotes of the seasons
he composes his undead corpse

above the passage of his birth
he draws what light there is

he gathers the song of his lover
which is perfumed and winged

its desire is for spring to return
rushing through his veins

not from north, south, east or west
but from a fifth direction

dark, green and glowering

Tom Pow

موقف البحـر

أجتاحُ في انقضاضي
أسطورةَ الأبيضِ والبياضِ
وعندَما تكتملُ السكينة
وتصبحُ الموجةُ نقشاً عارياً
في جسدِ السفينة
أجمعُ نبضي كلَّه
في طلقةِ المخاضِ
وأبدأُ انتفاضي

The Sea

with swell after swell
I quell the white myth
till calmness is complete

and the wave carves
a naked inscription
on the body of the boat

I gather all that throbs
within me
to me

with the first
rip tide of labour
I begin to tremble and shake

Tom Pow

Zuhair Abu Shaib

اسـم التـراب

ما اسمُه ؟
ما اسمُ هذا الترابِ الّذي هرَّ
من جسدي المتساقط ؟
ما اسمُه حين هرَّ
وحين تكوّمَر تحتَ ثيابي
ولبّنتُه حائطاً إثرَ حائط ؟

لي سماءٌ أغيّمُها
أدّعيها كما شئتُ
أشهقُ ملءَ الينابيع في ليلها
ثمّ ألقفُها حين تهفتُ بالأنبياءِ
ضيوفاً عليَّ
وأسألُهم :
الّذي حبسَ الروحَ في حجَرٍ ،
والّذي فيّضَ الأنبياءَ على عتّباتِ البيوتِ
كليمُ الترابِ
المُغيرُ على كلِّ شيْءٍ لينهبَه
والمحدّقُ في ظلّه كغريبِ
ما اسمُه ؟
وطني أم بدايةُ منفايَ
معجزتي أم صليبي ؟
ما اسمُه ؟

Name of the Soil

what is its name?
what is the name of the soil
          that falls from my withered body?
what is its name as it drifts and gathers
                              under my clothes
while, slowly, I build wall after wall?

I picture a sky full of clouds
I see it as I wish it to be

when night falls, I gulp my fill of springs
in the darkness I lift my latch
to wise men

I ask my guests
who imprisoned the soul in rock?
who left prophets spreadeagled on doorsteps?

who risks everything to capture the earth?
a man who does not know his own shadow

what can I call this rug of soil?
is it my country or the source of my exile?
is it my miracle or my cross?

what is its name?

Tom Pow

اسـم التراب

ما اسمُه ؟
ما اسمُ هذا الترابِ الّذي هرَّ
من جسدي المتساقط ؟
ما اسمُه حين هرَّ
وحين تكوّمَ تحتَ ثيابي
ولبّنتُه حائطاً إثرَ حائط ؟

لي سماءٌ أعيّمُها
أدّعيها كما شئتُ
أشهقُ ملءَ الينابيعِ في ليلِها
ثمّ ألقَفُها حين تهفِتُ بالأنبياءِ
ضيوفاً عليَّ
وأسألُهم :
الّذي حبسَ الروحَ في حجَرٍ ،
والّذي فيّضَ الأنبياءَ على عتّباتِ البيوتِ
كليمُ الترابِ
المُغيرُ على كلِّ شيْءٍ لينهبَه
والمحدّقُ في ظلّه كغريبٍ
ما اسمُه ؟
وطني أم بدايةُ منفايَ
معجزتي أم صليبي ؟
ما اسمُه ؟

Ainm na talmhainn

Ciod e a h-ainm?
Ciod e ainm na talmhainn seo a' tuiteam bho mo bhodhaig, a' tuiteam às a
chèile?
Ciod e a h-ainm fhad 's a thuiteas i agus a chruthaicheas i fo mo chuid
aodaich
Fhad 's a thogas mi balla an dèidh balla?

Tha adhar agam, cuiream neul air
Gur leam e mar mo mhiann
Òlam na lìon an t-allt tron oidhche
agus an sin, glacaidh mi e fhad 's a thuiteas e leis na fàidhean.
Agus mo chuid aoighean a' nochdadh,
's tha mi a' faighneachd dhaibh:
Cò ghlas an t-anam anns a' chreig?
Agus cò dhòirt na fàidhean air na starsaichean?
Brat na h-ùire
An creachadair a chreachas gach nì airson a ghoid
Fear a' sgrùdadh fhaileas fhèin, mar gum bu choigreach dha e.

Ciod e a h-ainm?
Mo dhùthaich fhìn no toiseach m' fhògraidh?
Mo mhìorbhail no mo chrann-ceusaidh?
Ciod e a h-ainm?

Gillebride MacMillan

Bisan Abu Khaled

بيسان أبو خالد

لم يعد في قصائد بوشكين

شيء سيدهش لينين
واجه مصيرك ياأيها العشق .. لاتنتحر
ولا زمن سوف يمهل أي حبيبين كي ننتظر
بعد أول قبلة
و اخر موعد
دقائق تنحر كل النساء إذا لم يطفن بطيف الحنين
و لا أحد سوف يبصر
أو سوف يعرف أن خرائط كوكبنا زيّفت وجه نجمتنا التي حملت دائما اسمها
واسمها الآن يبقى فلسطين
أغنيتي ... وبلادي ... ووجهي الحزين

Not Considered in Poems of Pushkin

Lenin thought the world could be a homeland
without boundaries for all. O loved one,
face bad things he did not foresee.
Minutes erode all women, even those
not first bled down to a dry ghost by
nostalgia, our vampire bat.
Will one day none see on a new faked map
the name of she who is mine,
my loved homeland, Palestine?

Alasdair Gray

Bisan Abu Khaled
Bridge translations by Telche Hanley-Moyle

What Pushkin's poems never said

Something that will startle Lenin -
oh love, confront your destiny – don't kill yourself.
Time will not slow down for lovers to tarry
after the first kiss
and the last time they met.
Passing minutes would slit the throats of the women
had they not already drowned themselves in nostalgia.

Shall no one bear witness or know
that the maps of our planet have lied
about the face of our star
which always used to show her name.

Her name is and always was Palestine
My song...
my homeland...
my face full of sorrow.

Magi Gibson

امرأة النسيان

هنا امرأة المطر اليوم تظهر
من ذاكرات الشتاء
تكفكف جرح التسعع في نزف هذا اللهاث و تُوقفني
عند أسئلة خلتها تتآكل بعد الجوابْ ..
هنا رجل يتواجه و امراة في كتاب
فأيهما كان أكثر حبرا ... و كان أكثر نزفاً
وأيهما قد يشح انتظارا لفهرسة المكتبات
ومذ عدت من أغنياتي عجبت
سالومي تدحرج رأسا على سفح هذا العدم
تريد لسيزيف أن يحمل الان صخرته
وجه ما قد تبقى لنا من ملامحه المعمدان
تجرأ أن يرفض الرقص
تحت ظلال الجريمة و الشمعدان
يهودية تتصهين في نصلة
وتطيح برأس الحقيقة بالصولجان

Woman of Forgetfulness

Here, today, the rain woman appears
from memories of winter,
wiping at her wanderer's wounds, breath bleeding from her in gasps, and
she stops me
at questions I thought vanished into answers:

here, a man and a woman face each other in a book—
which of them is more ink, and which more blood?
Which of them will wither while waiting
for the libraries to be indexed?

Returning from my songs, I am astonished:
Salome rolls a head to the foot of this void,
demanding Sisyphus carry his rock now,
his face tracing remnants of the Baptist's
who dared refuse dancing
in the shadow of a crime and a menorah—
a Jewish woman Zionised into a blade,
beheads the truth with a sceptred blow,
while oak ships beget ships,
and I sail on the froth of ink and blood,
between this moment and your last, O lady of death—between the dignity
of silence
and the vulgarity of sound

so that before our bodies find refuge in the grave
they may reveal a woman

Bisan Abu Khaled

ground beneath the millstone of war
refusing confession, refusing
the illusion of prayer before death
and the letters P and B will condense the echo
of a woman shunning the indignity of tears,

and in her travels P and B,
Palestine and Beirut,
distilled into the essence of ruin,
become bywords for war

and nothing resembles the woman of ink and blood so much as a country
that, once upon a siege, would leave its capital gloriously standing
mirrored in a mockery of steadfastness
while we are dying...

A country will choose this madness
unless we say we are returning.

Amal El-Mohtar

يوسف عبـد العزيـز

كتـاب الشّـك

الليلةَ
صادفتُ العزلةَ في البيتِ
وقد لبست أجملَ قمصاني،
كانت تشربُ مِن قَهوَتي المُرَّة
أيضاً
وتدخِّنُ تبغي،
وتقلِّبُ ما يشبهُ مخطوطاً لي.
كانت تجلسُ في كرسيِّ
مِثلَ الملكاتِ
وبين يديها
غيمٌ مجنونٌ يتطايرُ ...

مُتشحاً برؤايَ وقفتُ قريباً منها
كنتُ هناك أرقُّ كغصن الليلِ
وأهطلُ بالأسئلةِ
المُرَّة :
ما المرأةُ ؟
في أيّةِ عاصفةٍ يمكنُ
أن يلعبَ قلبي ؟
أين دفنتُ النار ؟!

وكأنّي خاتَمُ إصبعها
لم تبصرني ،
لم تبصر ظلّي المتيبِّسَ قربَ البابِ

Yousef Abdul-Aziz
Bridge translations by Lauren Pyott

The Book of Doubt

Tonight
I stumbled across Solitude in my house.
Not only wearing my best shirt
and drinking my coffee
but also
smoking my tobacco
it was thrashing about the pages
of what looked like my manuscript.
It sat in my chair like a queen
and from its hands
rose an enchanted fog…

Still cloaked in my dreams I stood close by
trembling like a branch of the night
raining down bitter
questions:

> What is woman?
> In which storm
>   may my heart play?
> Where did I bury the fire?!

As though I were a ring on its finger
it didn't give me much thought.
Unfazed by my stiff shadow at the door

وواصلت العزلة
لعبّ الدّورِ السّاخر
أخذت تُمسِكُ أوراقاً
وتمزّقها من ذاك المخطوط،
فكنت أراني مقذوفاً لبرارٍ عمياءَ
أصيحُ
أمامي طابةُ ماءٍ
تعلو في الرّيح ،
وفوقي قمرٌ يتشقّقُ
ويحطُّ كرِفُّ فراشٍ مقتولٍ
قربي

لا بُدَّ لخاتمةٍ
تنهي هذي الملهاةَ صرختُ
فحدّقتِ العزلةُ فيَّ بعيني ظبيٍ
كانت عينيَّ
وألقت نحوي
بكتاب الشَّكِّ فكانَ كتابي.

Solitude went on
with a sneer
scrambling pages
tearing them out of the manuscript.
I saw myself cast out to blind lands
and I hollered;
I saw before me a sphere of water
rising up in the wind
and above, a cracked moon,
and slain butterflies
strewn around me.

I'm sure
you will soon wrap up this farce! I yelled.
Solitude glanced at me with its two eyes of a gazelle—
my own eyes.
And it handed me
the book of doubt—it was my own book.

Juana Adcock

Yousef Abdul-Aziz

The Buik o Doot

The nicht,
A stottert ower Solitude in ma hoose.

Wearin ma best shirt,
it wis drinkin fae ma bitter coffee
an smokin ma baccie.

It wis makin a boorach
o whit luiked like ma manuscript,
sittin in ma chair,
the wey a queen dis.
An fae atween its hauns
a mad haar wis gan up.

Clothit in ma visions, A stuid close by.
There A wis, tremblin lik a branch o the nicht,
rainin doon bitter questions:

Whit is this wumman?
Which storm cin ma hairt play?
Whaur did A bury the fire?

As if A wis a ring oan its finnger
it didnae gie me muckle thocht
it wisnae bothert aboot ma rigid shadda by the door.

An Solitude cairriet oan
playin the satirical role.

It stertit grabbin at papers,
tearin them fae thon verra manuscript.
A seen masel chuckt oot tae the blin lans
an A screkkit.

Afore me wis a baw o watter
risin up in the win,
an abuin me, a muin splittin
an placin itsel lik a group o murdert butterflees
aside me.

Nae doot,
thir is an enn tae this farce A skrekked.

Solitude starit at me wi twa doe een.
They wir ma ain een
An it flung agin me.
The Buik o Doot, it wis ma ain buik.

Liz Niven

الحظيـرة

لمّا رجعتُ لمنزلي متأخّراً في الليلِ.

عادَ ليَ ارتباكي

مثلَ كيسِ الرّملِ كانّ المنزلُ الحجريُّ منبطحاً، وكنتُ أرى نوافذَهُ المضيئةَ كالثُّقوبِ، وكانتِ الأزهارُ فوقَ السُّورِ ترفعُ في الظّلامِ رؤوسَها كأصابعِ الأعمى.

اقتربتُ فمالتِ الجدرانُ نحوي، وارتجفتُ كأنّني أهذي، كأنّي خارجَ الحجرِ المرتّبِ في نشيدِ الصّمتِ أُطلِقُ من يدي طيرَ الحواسِّ واستفزُّ النّارَ تحتَ رمادِها.

حرّكتُ رأسي في فضاءِ اللغزِ مثلَ الأرنبِ المذعورِ، هذا البيتُ بيتي ، فيه أعجنُ من رمادِ الرّوحِ قلبَ الشّعرِ، أرفعُ بُرجَ أحلامي وأصعدُهُ لكي أطأَ السّحابَ الرّخوَ، هذا البيتُ بيتي، غيرَ أن السّقفَ يوشكُ أن يطيرَ، ويوشكُ الشُّباكُ أن يهوي عليَّ مصفِّقاً كالنّسرِ، هذا البيتُ بيتي؟ السّورُ نفسُ السّورِ؟ لا قد صارَ أعلى، والحجارةُ فيهِ تبدو مثلَ أسنانٍ مهزّأةٍ.

دفعتُ البابَ مُرتبكاً فأنّتْ في ظلامِ الليلِ جثّتُهُ، وهبّتْ باتجاهي الرّيحُ مُثقلةً برائحةِ العفونةِ، خطوةً ووقفتُ، يا اللهُ أيّةُ لحظةٍ تلقي عليّ غموضَها؟!

ثورانِ مثلَ غمامتينِ ترنّحا في البابِ، روثٌ يغمرُ الأرجاءَ، كانَ البيتُ نصفَ مهدّمٍ، ومضيتُ في حجراتِهِ، غنمٌ وأبقارٌ على السّجّادِ تلهو أو تنامُ، على الأرائكِ تجلسُ القطط الكسولةُ، كانت الحمّى بألفِ يدٍ تدقُّ ضلوعيَ الخرساءَ والأصواتُ تصعدُ في العروقِ وتضربُ الصّدغينِ، حينَ مضيتُ إلى سريري كان قُرّادٌ يحطُّ عليَّ يلسعُني فأصرخُ صامتاً، شَعرٌ غزيرٌ صارَ ينبتُ فوقَ أعضائي وحينَ نظرتُ في المرآةِ لم أرَ ما يدلُّ عليَّ، كنتُ شبيهَ تيسٍ هائلٍ، فذهبتُ صوبَ النّافذةِ وبدأتُ أثغو.

The stable

When A got back hame, late at nicht, ma bamboozlement came back tae me.

Lik a bag o saun the stane hoose lay doon. A cuid see its windaes lit up lik perforations an the flooers oan the waas liftit thir heids in the derk lik a blin man's finngers.

A goat closer an the waas leant in oan me. A shook as if in a dwam; as if A wir ootside the stane arranged in the sang o silence, A let oot fae ma haun a burd o the senses an lichtit the fire ablow the ashes. A shook ma heid in the void o the riddle lik a feart rabbit.

This is ma hoose.

In it A knead the hairt o poetry fae the ash o the soul. A raise up the tooer o ma dreams an sclimb so A can step ontae shilpit cloods.

This is ma hoose.

Even if the roof is aboot tae flee an the windaes ur aboot tae faw doon oan me, clappin lik an eagle, this is ma hoose.

These are thae same waas

It has raisit nae higher, an the stanes inside it seem lik rotten teeth. A pusht the door, confused, an its boadie moaned in the derkness o the nicht.

Yousef Abdul-Aziz

The win blew agin me, thick wi the reek o decay. Wan step an A stoappt. Oh god, whit a meenit stammygastert me.

Twa bulls wir lik twa cloods stottin throu the door, thir droppins littert aw aroon. The hoose wis hauf wreckt. A past alang its stanes, yowe an kye oan the carpets. Dauncin aboot or sleepin. Oan the settees sat lazy cats. The fever straik in ma mute ribs wi a thoosan hauns, vyces got up in ma veins an chappit oan ma foreheid.

When A goat tae ma bed, flees set aboot me, bitin me. A let oot a quate scream. Muckle herr had stertit tae grow aw ower ma limbs an gin A seen masel in the mirror, A seen nae sign o mascl.

A wis the ghaist o a wappin great billy-goat, sae A went tae the windae an stertit tae bleat.

Liz Niven

عبد الرحيم الشيخ

عنوانٌ واحدٌ للبـريد

في طريقي إليهمْ أمرُّ بهِ
في طريقهِ إليهمْ يمرُّ اللهُ بيْ
ولا يرى اثنانا سواهمُ عندما نفترقْ
هُمُ الأعلى

وحدهم يُمْضُونَ ليلَهُم الأبْدْ
يتقاسمونَ أسِرَّةً من أرجوانِ الفجرِ قبلَ الإنفجارْ
يتناثرونَ على حدودِ الشوكةِ الكبرى، فلسطين، انتظاراً للنَّدى
لا وردَ إلا هُمْ عليها

منهمُ، الواقفين على شفيرِ الجنةِ الأُولى /
ومنْ حكاياتِ الصغارِ الراسمينَ خريطةً بالشوكِ فوقَ الجنةِ الأُولى، ومنها،
سوفَ نبني في سماءِ اللهِ قوساً للعبادةِ، قِبْلَةً أُولى .. وقُبْلَةْ
للذينَ يغادرونَ بلا حقائبَ أو وثائقَ للعبورْ

همُ العبورْ .. متعمِّدينَ، كما الحقيقةِ، هَهُنا
تركوا حقائبَهم بريدٌ مِنْ أكَفِّ اللاحقينْ
واللاحقونُ سيتركونَ بريدَهم كالأوَّلينَ .. بريدُنا صعبُ الوصولِ لجنَّةٍ أخرى، ولا
عُنوانَ خارجَ سُرَّةِ الدُّنيا، هنا، أبداً سيعرفُهُ البريدْ .

Abdel Rahim al-Sheikh
Bridge translations by Lauren Pyott

Single Address for the Post

On my way to them, I pass Him by,
(as, on his way, God passes me by)
for as we go our separate ways
we see no one but those on high.

The beds are allotted before the violet dawn.
The black and endless night is spent alone
and then the cataclysm comes

that will seed them from the borders of Palestine
the Great Thorn.
They are the only roses that grow.

From where they stalk the edge of paradise
the first paradise.

From where the children use thorns
to draw maps of this paradise.

From this spot.

We raise in the sky a glorying arc
the first milestone to Mecca

Abdel Rahim al-Sheikh

and we leave a kiss for those who left
with neither luggage nor papers for their passage.

This is the way the journey will always be.
They leave their bags for the postman to deliver

He takes them from the hands
of those who follow

And those who follow leave their packages
as the first ones do.

It's hard for the post to make it to paradise.
There is no address
neither here nor there.

Rachel McCrum

غَسَــق

ها وحدَهُ طائرُ الليلِ .. وَحْدَهْ، يُعِدُّ شمسَ أيارَ لجناحيهْ
يسبقُ الشرقَ إليها، يؤثِّثهُ بها، ثم يمضي غاسلاً طرَفَ الأعالي، قيثارةُ الريشْ
يعرفهُ الأحبَّةُ برمشينِ شُدَّا لبرقُصا رغبةَ البهلوانِ، قدميهِ، على حبلٍ من مسدْ
أسودانِ، وكلُّ شيءٍ زائلٌ إلاهُ، وغالقُ الكاميرا، وألوانُ قزَحْ ... سرمدٌ لا سوءَ فيهْ
لم يكن سادنَ الليلِ يؤذِّنَ في الناسِ، صُبحاً، أنْ آتيةٌ في المغيبِ بقيةُ الليلْ
كانَ بقيةَ الصبحِ فيهمْ ، قيثارةَ الريشِ كانَ ... وكانْ، «عاشقاً سيءَ الحظْ»
حظاً سيءَ العشقِ، ملتقيَّ، نهراً ونازْ، ضفَّةً في الخارجِ الكلِّيِّ ثالثةً
لم يكن صبّاً يناورُ ... يثبتُ بالنهدِ كرويةَ الأرضْ
لم يكن يدحو فَراشَّتَهُ فِراشاً للتي ستئنُّ، أثناهُ النعاشْ
حلمهُ وجعٌ تقدَّمَ ، لا خرائط للعبورِ تقولُ للوادي انتبهْ :
ها طفلٌ بحركَ خالعٌ نعليهِ، متكِئٌ على جبلِ القمرْ
برزخٌ متباعدٌ الخطواتِ، أزرقُهُ ارتواءٌ، لؤلؤُهُ مؤجَّلْ
يا لنارهْ ! يا لنايهْ !
يا لـ«تبديلِ العوالمِ» /
والعوامِلِ في تحوُّلِهِ الأخيرْ!

Dusk

there is a bird, alone… alone and measuring the may sun with the
beating of his wings,
more eager than the east, he grooms, speeds past, clips the mountain
crest, a feather harp,
known to lovers by his eyelashes, his fierce dance, his acrobat desire, on
raffia rope, his two black feet,
and all is fleeting but him, the camera shutter, the full rainbow… a
world without end or sorrow,
and he is not the night warden, does not tell each morning of the night
returning at sunset,
as the night will always return, and the feather harp… a lover out of a
luck and a luck out of love,
a meeting point, a river, a fire, a brink of all things, again and again and
again,
his feints and flits are far from tender… he settles on her breast, as
round as the world,
holding in his butterflies, a blanket for the grieving, his partner in sleep,
and his dreams are aches which march onward, and there are no maps
for the crossing, and she warns him:
that child, your sea, is taking off his shoes, is leaning on the mountains
of the moon,
a strait where paths break, a quenching blue, a clouded pearl…
oh his fire! oh his flute!
oh the changing world…
and who executes the final turn!

Harry Giles

سمـيـح فــرج

هُنـا أمجد
(إلى الشهيد أمجد فرج الذي ناضل ضد الاحتلال حتى أدركه المرض وربما..)

هُنا أمجدْ
هُنا بيّارةُ الليمونِ نَستهدي بنكهتها
ومَن يَستأنسُ الليمونَ لا يخبو
ولا يتعبْ
هُنا بيارةُ الليمون نَستجلي
فتأخذنا إلى الأشهى
وتحْملنا إلى الأبعدْ

هُنا تستيقظُ الأيّامُ مِنْ لحمٍ
ومنْ دمنا
هُنا نشقى
هُنا نبقى
هُنا إيقاعنا العالي
هُنا «بُرِّشْ»
هُنا عَرِّشْ
يُقلِّبُ في صبيحتِهِ
قُصاصات
ويقرأُ صُوتها العاني
ويَفتحُ بابها الأوحدْ
ولـ«الكتسيم»
حَسراتٌ وخشرَجةٌ

Samih Faraj
Bridge translations by Lloyd Randle

Here Lies Amjad
(To the martyr Amjad Faraj who stood against the
occupation until illness took him, and perhaps something
else…)

Here lies Amjad

Here lies a lemon grove

We are steered by its bright bitter smell

Carrying lemons means you cannot die
or grow tired

Here lies a lemon grove we weed and dig
till it has made us happy as children
and carried us miles away

Here lie the days that grow from our flesh
grow from our blood

Here we mourn

Here we stay

Here is our greatest battle
Here is a mat

هُنا أمجدْ
لقد أَسقيت مَنْ أَسقيت يا أمجدْ
لقد أَسقيت مَن غضبوا
ومَن قرأوا
ومَن كتبوا، يحب الناسُ أَنْ تبقى
نُعبِّئ صفحة أُخرى بنرجسها
يشاءُ اللهُ أَنْ تَصعدْ
هُنا لُغزٌ
وفلسفةٌ
هُنا الفردوسُ في المشهدْ
هُنا الأمجدْ..

Here is a chair

Leafing through the morning
stories
he follows their fierce sound
and opens their singular door

- by God –
Shaping breath
of pain, death knocking
in the throat

Here lies Amjad

You have watered everyone, Amjad
Slaked the thirst of everyone
who became angry
everyone who read
everyone who wrote

The people want you to stay
filling the blank soil of another page
with radiant flowers
God wills you to flower again

Here lies a riddle
and a philosophy
Here lies paradise
in place of a grave

Here lies Amjad

Ellen McAteer

سَيِّدةٌ

دَرَجٌ
يَتَسَلَّلُ نحو المنزلِ
أو يهبطُ نحو الدارْ
سَيِّدةٌ تجلسُ، والوقتُ مساء، كانت
في يَدِها سُبّحةٌ
وَرَفيفُ حَمامٍ، ومشاهدُ، لا أحدٌ يَعرفُ
في أيِّ بعيدٍ كانت تمضي
أو تذهبُ في أيِّ مدارْ
لا أحدٌ
في أيِّ غِمارٍ كانت تدخلُ
أو تخرجُ مِنْ أيِّ بِحارْ
سَيِّدةٌ
دَرَجٌ
والأرضُ قِفارٌ
إلا مِنْ دَمِنا المُتسلِّقِ
كُلُّ الأحلامِ حِصارْ

A Woman

Take one step towards the old house
And another down the stairs to the home
Where a woman sits in the early evening light:
Light, the radiance of a dove, shining;
Or light like the light from a shrine.
No one knows where she has come from -
Through which quarter or distant land she passed.
No one knows which door she opened -
What shadow the light cast when she'd gone.
No one knows the flood she passed through -
The risks she took, the daily deluge.
No one can measure the vast sea she crossed,
The hazards she held in her small hands.
An ordinary woman: one step at a time, one step
On the land lacking, on the barren soil; one step
On the time passing; one step on the clock ticking.
Except for something in her now rising, hot, scolding.
Even her dreams are besieged, it seems; yet
In the middle of a siege it's still possible to dream.
A dream of the old house, and her first step.

Jackie Kay

سميـة السوسي

العـارفـة

طرق نافذةٍ هشة، يصاحب نغمةً
تخريش جداريات الكلام،
كائن الصباح يدرك جيداً
كيف يسرق النوم ببراعة قِطٍّ
لا يترك مساحة للمزيد من الاختباء،
ضوء ما، أحمر ربما، أو صباحي عنيد،
يفتح عين الصبية على وقت لا يدركه ليل أو نهار
وقت غرائبي للعبث الجميل بثنايا النوم
المعلَّق بأجفان الكلمات،
يضيف ما يلزم تماماً

يا العارفة بكِ:
أناديكِ صهيلاً في أجنحة الرقة
لنتم المشوار

يا العارفة بي:
أضيئي شموع الحلاوة
لليلٍ يشتاق إلى
رائحة التراب
يا العارفة به :
ضمّي إليكِ خوف الروح،
لن يحتملَ برد الصباح
على كتفيه، شدي غطاءك أكثر
اغمريه ،اغمريه

Somaya Al-Susi
Bridge translation by Shabana Basheer

Knowing

He raps his knuckles on the frost-thin panes,
crackling percussion for this melody.
She scratches out a verbal fresco,
code for dwellers in his own familiar dawn.
He knows how to steal a twist of your sleephood
with the skill of a cat.

And he leaves behind no nook for hidden things
but instead, just a little light (maybe it's red, and
maybe headstrong, like my kind of morning).

She opens one eye in the half-dark of day-spun night.
Eerie twilight is a time for teasing dances
uncurling from the folds of sleep
and hanging there, crept in the eyelids of each word
as it opens.
It's just what I need.

And oh, how I have come to know you.
I send my winged howl to you across the air
on its own flight plath, meeting
at our journey's end.

And oh, how you have come to know me:

يفوح ملاكاً وخاتمَ نور

الليل،

حين نربطه قليلاً بساقية الخرافة،

يتأخر

هل يحتمل لقيانا ؟

لنتذوق بعضاً من تمر الحكاية

ولحنها الجنوبي

يا العارفة بنا:

رحيمة أنتِ

بكل روح تشق بذرتها

لتكتمل.

you light me little sweet-smelling candles
as offerings to night (though we remember
that the night prefers the scent of soil).

Oh, what it is to know him.
Admit that you're afraid of ghosts.
I've learned that he can't stand the cold of early dawns.
It ices his shoulders. So cover him,
cover him, pull your blanket over him tighter.
You will see that he emits a kind of light,
and you see it is the light of angels,
the kind of light that only comes from night.
We see it glimmer in the eddies
sparking from the water wheel in our old stories.

But he is late. Will he even come to meet me here?
Will he say that we can taste the dates
that we remember from our fairytales
on mornings that illuminate old myths,
and hear the southern songs we sang?
Oh, what it is to know the two of us.

My girl, I have seen that you love every life
that splits itself apart from seed
until it's whole, until it's done.

Charlotte Runcie

56

عثمـان حسيـن

مخيـم بلـوك (٥)*

كان يجب عليّ الذهاب، قلت : كان يجب . البرابرة يحاصرون الوقت والمكان ، يحاصرون تلك الأنفاس اللاهثة في الزقاق المتفرع من خيبة الرحلة الطويلة. الانفجارات تتلاحق والخوف سيد الموقف. الخوف المبرر والمنتصب في وجه التاريخ بمفترقاته الشاسعة. يرصدوننا ونرصدهم ونحاصر مجدهم بضعفنا. قذائف الدبابات ورصاص الأسلحة الخفيفة وحقدهم ، جميعها تتدحرج أمام آلة الهدم .

سأذهب الآن. الأطفال الكثيرون، النصف نائمون يتعثرون ويسقطون أثناء تدافعهم من بيوتهم عند ساعة الفجر الأولى. البيوت التي ستسوى كلعنةٍ مفاجئة بعد لحظة واحدة.

... يحمل الأب أطفاله ويندفع كقذيفة خارج كومة الأسمنت التي ستصير بعد قليل جداً، آه لو لم أنسحب قبل لحظة منك، لظل «أحمد المنسي» تحت الكومة التي صارت، كأنني على موعد مع النسيان المبرر، أيضاً.

الساعة تجاوزت أول الفجر والقذائف تدك البيوت المتهالكة وآلة الهدم العمياء تتقدم صوب بيوت المخيم الغارقة في بؤسها.

لكنهم يفرضون شروط المعركة ويهندسون ملامحها ومع ذلك يتساقط الأعداء كثمرات فاسدة، رصاصات غاضبة تصرخ في وجوه جنودهم ، من أسلحة هزيلة.

... يشتد وطيس المعركة. مساجد المدينة تكبر بصوت واحد. تدعو مسلحي كافة الفصائل إلى الدفاع عن بلوك (٥) المتهم في جغرافيته، ويرجا الحراسة الإسرائيليين يغطيان جرحاهم بمزيد من النار. المساجد تواصل صراخها والمقاتلون يستحكمون في مواقعهم الطارئة وينشرون الرعب في ترسانة العدو

يزداد الضغط على ساكني المخيم ، آلاف الصُّدَف تملأ ساحة المعركة، كل واحد يحمل صدفته الملقاة تحت قدميه ويهرب إلى المجهول البيوت لم تعثر على صدفة واحدة ، كذلك الأشجار المشتعلة بصواريخ ضالة ،س لم تعثر على صدفتها، أيضاً، سكان المدينة يملأون الشوارع يجيئون ويذهبون دون غاية أو هدف، يشبهون أسوداً تدور حول نفسها في أقفاصها المنيعة. الانفجارات تصم الآذان. الخوف ما زال يملأ رؤوس الناس . والقلق يحدق في ملامحهم الباهتة، عتمة الفجر تعيد تشكيل القلق لديهم . سيارات الإسعاف تداهم توقعات البارود. أما ذهابي فقد كان مبرراً، حين تركت الشاشة ولحظة مسروقة تبصرها عيناك الجميلتان.

Uthman Hussein
Bridge translation by Sarah Irving

Camp Block 5

I have to go, I said: I have to. The barbarians are besieging time and
place, besieging this rapid breathing in the side-alleys of frustration's
long journey. Explosions ripple, fear controls the situation. Justified and
upstanding fear in the face of history at a great crossroads. They monitor
us and we monitor them and we besiege their glory with our weakness.
Tank shells and small-arms fire and their hatred, all these roll before the
demolition machines.

I will go now. Many children, half asleep and stumbling and falling as
you hurry them from their houses at the hour of dawn. Houses that will
be levelled like accusations in just a moment.

A father carries his children and rushes like a missile out of what
will shortly be a pile of cement, oh if he didn't draw back from you a
moment, he would still be Ahmed al-Munsi under the pile which his
house became, as if I had an appointment with justified forgetting as
well. The hour of dawn passes and shells pound the dilapidated houses
and the demolition machine bears down on the overwhelmed blocks of
the camp in their misery.

But they get into battle formations and set their faces and despite
everything their enemies fall like rotten fruit, angry bullets screaming
from meagre weapons into the soldiers' faces.

The heat of battle intensifies. The mosques of the city call with one
voice. They call militiamen of all factions to the defence of Block 5 as its
position is under threat, to the Israeli guard tower covering their wounded
with the glory of fire. The mosques continue crying and the fighters take
up contingency positions and spread panic among the enemy.

رِثـاء

يا عصيةُ
هل تخلصتِ من سخطك المبهم ؟ إذن :
علِّميني كيف أعبر الطرقات والمساجد وأثغو بالفاتحة
أمسكي يدي واضغطي على أصابعي النحيلة كي أصرخ فجأة
أمام العابرين وأدحرج اللعنات تحت أقدامهم
أيتها المنادي يا بهية
لِمَ تركتني للاشيء
وتركتِ لي قناعاً مثقوباً
تسربي أيتها السوائل
انفخي الرؤوس
واغرقي أيتها الأقنعة.

The pressure on the camp's residents increases, thousands fill the battlefield, everyone takes his chances on his feet and flees to the unknown, to the houses which haven't fallen, and the trees set ablaze by stray missiles which haven't fallen either, inhabitants of the city fill the streets, coming and going without intent or aim like lions circling in their ineluctable cages. Explosions silence the call to prayer. Fear still fills people's heads. Anxiety stares from their livid features, the darkness of dawn returns. Ambulances make raids between cloudbursts of gunpowder. And as I would have been justified in getting out, I left the screen and a stolen moment of foresight in your beautiful eyes.

Henry King

A Lament

Oh obstinate one,
are you done with your strange sulk? Listen:
tell me how to navigate the alleys and mosques and I'll bleat the Fatiha
Grab my hand and click my thin fingers. Make me cry out suddenly
in front of the people in the street as curses roll under their shoes.
Oh, caller, beautiful one,
why did you leave me with nothing?
You made me a mask full of holes.
Let the liquids pour in
Let the heads swell up
Let the masks flood

Henry Bell

مـراد السوداني

طفولـة

خُذاني
إلى مرقدِ الطّيرِ في الصُبْحِ
ووشوشةِ الزهرِ للنّهرِ
وسعفِ النخيلِ المُشاغِبْ
*

خُذاني
إلى سروةِ القريةِ العاليةْ
وتلك الخُطى «تتعفرثُ»
في باحةِ الوقتِ
قليلٌ من «الولدناتِ» تبقّى
أغانٍ على حائطٍ ساقطٍ
في الطريقْ
دموعي التي صافحتْ شجرةَ الحورِ
ليلاً
قيائرُ من صنعِ صاحِبنَا الحقلِ ..
رغيفٌ رهيفٌ على يدِّ جدّتِنَا
في الخوابي
ثيابي البسيطةُ ترتاحُ
فوقَ السياج / ..
دجاجُ العجوزِ التي أربكتنا صغاراً
كلامٌ بريءٌ تدحرجَ فوقَ المقاعدِ
للطالباتِ الجميلاتِ
وُريقاتُ تينٍ تيّبسنَ فوقَ الرفوفِ
دفوفُ نساءِ القبيلةِ

Murad al-Sudani
Bridge translations by Sarah Irving

Childhood

Take me, you two,
To the shrine where birds sing at morning
And blossoms whisper to the river
And the palm-fronds.

Take me
To the tall cypress in the village
And those 'devilish' footsteps pattering
In the courtyard of time.
Few childish things remain
Like songs on the tumbledown wall
Beside the road
And tears that shook the poplar tree
All night
A guitar made by our friend the field,
A small loaf in our grandmother's hand
In al-Khawabi
Where my simple robe hangs on the fence / …
The chickens belonging to the old woman
Who got us muddled up as youngsters
We sprawled on our chairs, talking harmlessly
About the beautiful schoolgirls
Leaves drying on the shelves
The tambourines of the tribeswomen

ثغثغنَ دلاًّ
شجيراتُ لوزٍ على مفرقٍ ضائعٍ
ينتحبْ
وطفلٌ تشهّى نداءَ الأبوّةِ :
يا ابني!
يصارعُ دمعتهُ
وانسحبْ ..
تُنادمهُ الأرضُ بالقمحِ في شهقةِ الطيرِ
تلهو على شجرٍ من ذهبْ
فناصفَها الجرحَ والبوحَ
ودندنَ أغنيةً ..
وذهبْ
وراحتْ مباهجهُ الفاتناتُ تسابقهُ العدوَ
تنادتْ مواجِعُهُ النائحاتُ
ونامتْ
على
ساعديهِ
الكتبْ

*

خُذاني
إلى ثرثراتِ الصبا
والصيدِ في البرِّ
مشاويرِنا المتعبةِ
إلى قمرٍ شاحبٍ في العلالي
وليلِ التصابي على جذعِ خرّويةٍ للكلامِ
هناكَ اكتشفتُ
حدائقَ ظُلْمٍ
وغربةَ عمرٍ
وطفلاً بلا هدهداتٍ يُسرنَمُ

63

Beat flirtatiously
The almond-trees at the lonely crossroads
Weep
And a child longs to hear his father cry:
My son!
He struggles with his tears
Then surrenders
With the wheat-field he drinks the cries of the birds
As they play in the golden trees
For the servants of earth are wounds and revelations
And the song hummed without words…
Then he left
And his joys went racing beside him
Mourners invoked his sufferings
And the books
Slept
In his arms.

§

Take me, both of you,
To the chatterings of childhood
To the hunt across the land
To our wearying chores
To the pale, high moon
And a night passed childishly, talking under the carob
There I discovered
The gardens of oppression
The alienation of age

ذئباً جريحاً ..
تُصفّقهُ الريحْ
*
خُذاني
إلى صُحبةٍ خادعةْ !
رفاق الدهاةُ
يجيئونَ في موعدٍ مالحٍ
يسرقونَ الهدوءْ ..

«أولئك (حُسّادي) فجئني بمثلهم !»
خُذاني
إلى مهبطِ الواديينِ
وقافلةِ النحلِ محفوفةً باليعاسيبِ
ووردٌ يقهقهُ نعسانَ
ويعضُ نساءٍ مع الفجرِ
يَحطِبْنَ أخشابَ أيامهنَّ
على الرّيقْ
والطريقْ ..
لم تَعدْ مثلما كنتُ أعرفُها
في الطفولةْ
سهلةً لمْ تَعُدْ ..
ولمْ تَعُدْ تشرحُ الخطوَ
للعابرينْ
*
خُذاني
إلى باحةِ الدار
وأمي التي تطحنُ الوقتَ رغماً
وتنثرُهُ ..
تتلهّى بأشياءَ من صُنعِها

And a childhood bereft of a rocking cradle
An injured wolf
Whipped by the wind.

§

Take me, the pair of you,
To deceptive friendship!
– My shrewd companions
Coming at a time of tears
To rob me of my peace of mind…

"Those who once envied me – bring me people like them!"

Take me
Where two valleys meet
And the caravan of bees is beset by dragonflies
A rose's sleepy laughter
A group of women at dawn
Gather the day's firewood
On an empty stomach
And the road is no longer
As I knew it in childhood,
Easy-going,
And doesn't make sense of my steps
To those passing…

§

نسيجاً من القشِّ ..
بعضَ الصواني
هدايا بسيطةً
تقول لجدّي الذي شَغَّفَ الناسَ بي :
سوفَ يكبرُ .. يعبرُ نهرَ الحياةِ
وحيداً كما جيءَ به ...
سأدعوهُ دوماً حبيبي ..
وأدعو لهُ عقبَ كلِّ صلاةٍ
ليحرسهُ اللهُ من أعينِ الحاسدينَ
وأحرسهُ بالتعاويذ
و(قل أعوذُ بربِّ الفلقْ .. وطه)
وما يتقدَّسُ من كلماتِ الأعالي ..
وأحشو مخدَّته بالرُقى
وأدعوهُ دوماً حبيبي
وجدّي بنظرتِه الماكرةْ
يكرِّرُ ضحكتهُ الساخرةْ
تدقُّ الترابَ عصاهُ
ويفصحُ لي عن رؤاهُ :
تعلَّم دروبَ النفاقِ ؛
لأنَّ الحياةَ تُرابحُ من نافقوها
ونقِّل فؤادكَ بين الترددِّ
والخوفِ
كي تأمنَ العيشَ فوقَ العقاربْ
«إليكَ عنّي فلستُ ممن إذا اتقى
عِضاضَ الأفاعي نامَ فوقَ العقاربِ»
تلوَّنْ كهذا الزمان الجميلِ
تُهيئ لكَ الأرضُ أبوابَها
ويأتيكَ من كلِّ فجٍّ عميقٍ
مرائونَ ؛ يدعونَ لكْ ..

Take me, you two,
To the courtyard of the house
And my mother who ground out the time regardless
And scattered it…
She took pleasure in things she made
Weaving from straw
Some wicker trays
As simple gifts
She says to my grandfather who made people love me:
He will grow… he will cross the river of life
Alone, just as he entered it…
I will always call him my dearest
And in my prayers I ask
That God keep him from envious eyes
I guard him with amulets
As it is said: I take refuge in God, who dispels the shadows of night,
In the 20th Surah
And in what is sanctified by the words of the Highest
I cast spells over his pillow
And always call him my dearest…
My grandfather with his wily look
Roared again and again with laughter
Beat the ground with his stick
And told me the way he sees things:
Practise hypocrisy, my boy,
Because in this life, the hypocrites win
Your heart swithers between hesitation
And fear
So you sleep safely among scorpions

لا عليكْ
تحفُّ بكَ الطيرُ
«من كلِّ جنس»
ويمشي المُنى في ركابكَ
وببابكَ .. وقوفاً ترى الغادرينَ
يهزّونَ ذيلَ التقرّبِ :
مرحباً سيدي !
كنْ محبّاً لنفسكَ
فالغيرُ أدرى بأحوالهمْ
وزوّجْ خيالك حبَّ التملّكِ
والنعمةِ الخالصة !؟

"Leave me be, I am not like those who fear
The snapping of snakes and the stings of scorpions"
Be vivid and various as this beautiful era
And earth will open her doors for you,
While hypocrites come to you out of deep pits
Imploring…
Birds of every kind
Will take you under their wings
Destiny walks at your side
Deceivers fall over each other to reach your door, saying:
Greetings, sir!
Love yourself
The others can look after themselves
And in your imagination, marry
The love of possession and true grace!

Henry King

محمد لافي

••• نقش (١)

وأُريد أن يتراجعَ المنفى كثيراً
أو قليلاً
أن أزيحَ منازلَ الشهداءِ من كأسي
ليحتلَّ الشرابُ الراش
وأُريد أن أحيا حياتي مثلَ كلَّ الناش !

تحذير
(إلى أحدهمْ)

في الصحو والمنامْ
إهْذِ كما تشتهي، ويشتهي
«تنظيمُكَ» / الكلامْ
لكن أقولُ في الختامْ
لا تقتربْ منّي ..
أنا المنطقةُ الحرامْ!

MOHAMMED LAFI
Bridge translations by Shabana Basheer

inscription

and often I want exile to be gone
or just relax
so I can chase the living martyrs from my glass
and feel the drink invade my conscious self
so I can live my life like everybody else

Jim Ferguson

warning
(for someone)

awake and asleep
blether away as you like   as they like
Your Organisation / its endless /endless speeches
force me to say
do not come near me…
I am forbidden territory!

Jim Ferguson

أنا والشبيه

لم يكن في المسار ليَ ابناً،
ولا والداً، أو أخاً، أو صديقاً
ولكنني ظلتُ أقرَأُهُ في الحضورِ،
وأقرأُهُ في الغيابِ،
وأقرأه كلّما عسكرت عادياتُ الزمانِ
على البابِ،
ظلتُ أهاتِفُهُ خفيةً وعلانيةً،
وأصيحُ به كلّما ضلّت الخطوات بنا
في ضواحي النضال البعيداتِ :
قِفْ يا مُحَمّدْ !
أرْخِ أُذْنَكَ لي، واستمِعْ جيّداً يا مُحَمّدْ !
إن عذريةً في ضميركَ لو خُدشت مرّةً
حرقت،
والذي سيصيرُ رماداً بدربكَ لن يتَجَدّدْ.
*

لم أكُ ابناً له في المسار، ولا والداً
أو أخاً، أو صديقاً، ولكنّه ظلّ لي
آخر المتبقين من أُسرَة الذئبِ،
يَحرسني إن غفوتُ،
ويتبعني إن مشيتُ،
ويعوي عليّ إذا ضاعَ منّي عشبُ الطريقِ
إلى البيتِ : قِفْ يا مُحَمّدْ !
أرْخِ أُذْنَكَ لي، واستمِعْ جيّداً يا مُحَمّدْ !
إن عذريةً في ضميركِ لو خُدشتْ مرّةً
حرقت،
والذي سيصيرُ رماداً بدربك لن يتَجَدّدْ.

my other self and I

my son doesn't walk this path with me
nor my father   or brother   or a friend
but I sense his presence as I walk
and I sense his absence as I walk
and whenever past misfortunes camp at the door
I sense his presence more
calling out in whispers and shouts
whenever our steps seem lost
on the edge of the war:
stop! Mohammed
open your ears and listen hard   O Mohammed!
if your innocent conscience is violated even once
it will turn to fire

on the path I am not a son for him   nor a father
a brother   or a friend   yet he remains with me
that last faithful survivor from the family of the wolf
watching guard over me at night
following me through the day
and he howls when I step off
of the grass that leads the way:
stop! Mohammed
open your ears and listen hard   O Mohammed!
the virginity of your conscience   once sullied
will burn
and the ashes on your path will never be reborn

Jim Ferguson

منام

على مدارِ ليلتين قبل «فجّةِ» النهارْ
شاهدتُ ساكني القبورْ:
أبي، وأُمي، زوجتي، أُختي، أخي الكبيرْ
يعانقونني على رصيف الانتظارْ
بينما المسافرون حولي ...
يصعدون للقطارْ !

اعتذارية
إلى ضريح شهيد

أحاول ألاّ أمرَّ عليكَ
لئلا تكاتبني شاهداتُ القبورْ
أحاولُ أن أستجيرْ
بآخر (لا) أورثها إليّ النسورْ
أحاولُ أن أبتدي من شوارعَ
ليستْ مطرّزة بالسكوتْ
أحاولُ ألاّ أموتْ

8/9/1989

dreams

in the long night before sun's rude wakening
I see my treasured dead:
my father and mother   my wife   my sister   my older brother
they hug me in the waiting room and on the platform
while other travellers ready themselves…
and board the train!

Jim Ferguson

apology
-   to a martyr's grave

I try not to pass you by

so the gravestones will not summon me
I try to seek protection
in the final NO of the eagles' cries
I try to start from the streets
streets embroidered with the echo of life
I try to live

Jim Ferguson

لوحات
«إلى أحمد أبو سليم»

ليلّياً
تنبتُ فوقَ جدارِ الغرفةِ منذ زمنْ
شطآنٌ ، ومناراتٌ، ومحيطاتٌ، وسُفُنْ
ووجوه أعرفها، أو لا أعرفُها
ساحاتٌ،
شرفاتٌ ساقطةٌ سهواً من وطنٍ ما
منذ زمنْ
ليلياً تتشكّلُ نفسُ اللوحاتِ، ولكنْ
- أبداً - ثمّة في أقصى كلٍّ منها
في الزاويةِ اليمنى .. نعشٌ وكفنْ !
حنان

في كلِّ ليلةٍ يرنُّ خطوُها
في البيتِ من جديدْ
من قال: إن ساكني اللحودْ
لا يحذفون ..
ما بين دورةِ الحياةِ والمماتِ ..
من حدود.
(1/6/2012)

portraits and paintings
(for Ahmad Abū Salīm)

every night
and for some time now
they spread across the walls of my room
across sea-fronts   lighthouses   oceans and ships
across known and unknown faces
public spaces
and our forgotten homeland's fallen balconies
for some time now
and every night the same portraits form, but
- always   in the far right-hand corner of each
resides… a coffin and a shroud!
Hanān

every night her foot-steps
echo through the house anew
and say: believe me   the dwellers in the tombs
do not eliminate
the boundaries
between the cycle of life and death

Jim Ferguson

لوحات
«إلى أحمد أبو سليم»

ليليّاً
تنبتُ فوقَ جدارِ الغرفةِ منذ زمنْ
شطآنٌ ، ومناراتٌ، ومحيطاتٌ، وسُفُنْ
ووجوه أعرفها، أو لا أعرفُها
ساحاتٌ،
شرفاتٌ ساقطةٌ سهواً من وطنٍ ما
منذ زمنْ
ليلياً تتشكّلُ نفسُ اللوحاتِ، ولكنْ
- أبداً - ثمّة في أقصى كلٍّ منها
في الزاويةِ اليمنى .. نعشٌ وكفنْ !
حنان

في كلِّ ليلةٍ يرنُّ خطوُها
في البيتِ من جديدْ
من قال: إن ساكني اللحودْ
لا يحذفون ..
ما بين دورةِ الحياةِ والمماتِ ..
من حدود.
(1/6/2012)

Picturs
for Ahmad Abū Salīm

Ilka nicht,
Nicht efter nicht,
They lowp ower the chaumer wa,
Strands and heidlands, lichthooses, seas, ships,
Faces I ken, or dinna ken,
Plazas,
Pletties, forleitit and faan frae some hameland
Lang, lang syne,
Ilka nicht, thae same picturs, but
– aye in the faurmaist richt haun neuk o ilk yin o them's…
A deid-kist and a shrood!

Hanan.

Ilka nicht her step dirls
Ben the hoose yince mair…
Wha says, 'Deed aye,
Them that's ablow the mools
Dinna ding doon the dyke
Atween the birl o life and daith.

James Robertson

يوسف المحمود

الأعـــداء

يَجيئونَ من آخرِ الأرضِ كي يَجلسوا بيْنَنا
يجيئونَ من آخرِ الرّيحْ
بهم مرضٌ وفَحيحْ
يجيئونَ من آخرِ الثلج
يجيئونَ .. رائحةُ القتل فيهم
سكاكينهم يقطرُ الدم منها
بهم هلعٌ
ماكرون تماماً
قاتلون تماماً
فخورونَ بالقتلِ .. شُرّابُ دمّ
فخورونَ بالظفرِ والنّابْ
فخورونَ أكثرَ بالوهمِ والأسلحةْ
يَجيئونَ كي يَحرقوا مَوْسمَ الوَرد فينا
ويلقوا علينا العذابْ
بهم هلعٌ / غربةٌ / مرضٌ ..
-كيف جاءوا لكي يجلسوا بيننا ؟

81

Yousef al-Mahmoud
Bridge translations by Jona Fras

Enemy

They come from all the ends of the earth to sit among us
they come from the ends of the winds
they bring sickness and a hissing like snakes
they come from the ends of the snows
they come smelling of death
they come with blood-dripping knives
they bring panic and terror
they are utterly not-to-be-trusted
they are utterly murderous
they are proud of their murders, they are drinkers of blood
proud of tooth and nail
even more proud of guns and treachery
they come to burn the love in our hearts
and turn it to torture and bitterness
they bring sorrow, terror, sickness…
How have they come to sit among us?

DM Black

أعـالي القرنفـل

بيتُها في أعالي القرنْفُل،
قربَ تلالِ الرياحْ ..
في المساءِ احتمينا به
حَذَرَ المدفعيّةِ والطّائرات

*

كانَ صَوتُ الرصاصِ يلاحقُ قهوتَنا
ويهشِّمُ بعض الكلامْ.
كان صوتُ الرصاصِ ونبحُ المدافعِ
يدنو من الوردِ خلفَ النوافذِ،
يدنو من الدّفءِ والماءِ
ويعضُّ الشظايا ترنُّ على الدرجِ الخارجيِّ،
وتسقطُ قربَ الرخامْ

*

بيتُها في أعالي القرنفُلِ
ها نحنُ فيهِ
احتمينا بهِ
وابتعدنا إذن عن عيونِ الجنود اليهود.

Above the Carnations

Her house is above the carnations
on the path to the wind-swept hills…
At evening we sought refuge there
watching out for the guns and the aeroplanes.

The crack of bullets followed our coffee
and smashed into our conversation.
The crack of bullets and the bark of artillery
came near to the flowers inside the windows
came near to the warmth and the water jug
debris clattered down the outside stairway
and fell towards the marble pavement.

Her house is above the carnations
there we were in it
we had sought refuge there
and so we moved to where the Jewish soldiers could no longer see us.

DM Black

Yousef al-Mahmoud

أعـالي القرنفـل

بيتُها في أعالي القرنْفُل،
قربَ تلالِ الرياحْ ..
في المساءٍ احتمينا به
حَذَرَ المدفعيّةِ والطّائرات

*

كانَ صَوتُ الرصاصِ يلاحقُ قهوتَنا
ويهشِّمُ بعض الكلامْ.
كان صوتُ الرصاصِ ونبحُ المدافعِ
يدنو من الوردِ خلفَ النوافِذِ،
يدنو من الدّفءِ والماءِ
وبعضُ الشظايا ترنُّ على الدرجِ الخارجيِّ،
وتسقطُ قربَ الرخامْ

*

بيتُها في أعالي القرنفُلِ
ها نحنُ فيهِ
احتمينا بهِ
وابتعدنا إذن عن عيونِ الجنودِ اليهود.

Abuin the carnations

Her hoose is abuin the carnations
close tae the bens o the win
In the nicht we socht a safe bield in it
Watchin oot fir artillery an airplanes

The soond o bullets jinked wir coffee
an shattert some o wir wirds
The soond o bullets an bark o cannons
came near tae the flooers ahint the windaes
came near tae the hoose's warmth an the pitcher o watter
An some o the shards wir clatterin oan the ootside sterrs
fawin doon tae the marble

Her hoose is abuin the carnations
Thir we are in it.
We socht a safe bield in it
An hid fae the Jewish sodger's een.

Liz Niven

أبو حيـان بخطّ يـده

مالي إذا أمشي قليلاً أو كثيراً
تنقلبْ فوقَ خُطايْ.
مالي .. أنا البحرُ المحيطُ
يخونُني نجمي وتصفعُني يداي.
مالي ..
تضيقُ الأرضُ بي
وتغلّقُ الأبوابُ دوني
والذي لي ظلَّ يأخذه سوايْ.
*
أنذا وطيرُ النّحسِ فوقَ الرأسِ يزعقُ
منذ أن رقصت شموس الله فوقَ ضُحى صباي.
قلبي تعبّهُ الدموعُ وينفَلق
فوق الحصى
مالي إذن؟
وأنا المحيطُ . أنا المحيطُ
وحبّةُ الرّمل الصغيرةِ همر سوايْ.

Abu Hayyan in his own Hand-writing

What's wrong with me? whether I walk much or little
my footsteps keep toppling above me
what's wrong with me? I am the All-Encompassing Ocean
my star deceives me and my hands keep hitting me
the ground is too narrow for me to stand on
I am absent the gates of wisdom are closing
and that which belongs to me – someone other than me has run off with it.

Already when the suns of Allah danced in the morning of my youth
alrcady the bird of ill omen screeched above my head.
Tears burden my heart it is torn apart
above the pebbles.
What's wrong with me?
I am the Ocean. I am the Ocean
and the little grains of sand are other than me.

DM Black

أبو حيّان بخطّ يـده

مالي إذا أمشي قليلاً أو كثيراً
تنقلبْ فوق خُطايْ.
مالي .. أنا البحرُ المحيطُ
يخونُني نجمي وتصفعُني يداي.
مالي ..
تضيقُ الأرضُ بي
وتغلِّقُ الأبوابُ دوني
والذي لي ظلَّ يأخذه سوايْ.
*

أنذا وطيرُ النّحسِ فوقَ الرأسِ يزعقُ
منذ أن رقصت شموس الله فوقَ ضُحى صباي.
قلبي تعبُّهُ الدموعُ وينفَلق
فوق الحصى
مالي إذن؟
وأنا المحيطُ . أنا المحيطُ
وحبّةُ الرّمل الصغيرةِ همر سوايْ.

Abu Hayan in His Ain Haunscrievin

Whit's up wi me if A walk a wee bit or a lot?
Ma steps are gan heelstergoudie ower me.
Whit's up wi me? A'm the 'Encircling Sea'.

Ma stern is betrayin me an ma hauns ur scuddin me
Whit's wrang wi me?
A'm aw pitchert
An the doors ur shuttin wi'oot me
An the yin that's mine his been taen by someboadie else

Thon time, the burd o mishanter wis skrechin abuin ma heid
Since the suns o God dauncit abuin the morn o ma youth
Ma greetin hairt, is bein riven apairt
Abuin the stanes
Whit's wrang wi me then?
An A'm the Ocean. A am the Ocean
An the wee grain o saun is no me.

Liz Niven

سامي مهنا

نافذة

بيني وبين الصبحِ
نافذةٌ
أصادقُ نسمةً
ووشاحَ أُفْقٍ
تسردُ الغيماتِ قصةَ موعدٍ
فأصافحُ الوقتَ الجميلْ

بيني وبين الحُبِّ
نافذةٌ
أُطِلُّ على الربيعِ بعينِ
مَن عشقَ الزهورَ
ولوّعتْ أحلامَهُ
أحلامُها عندَ الرحيلْ

بيني وبين اللهِ
نافــذةٌ
أُسمّيها الجليلْ

SAMI MUHANNA
Bridge translations by Jona Fras

A Window

Between the sunrise and me there's a window.
So I greet my old friends the morning air
and the horizon's pencilled line. Those clouds
are gossiping about a secret rendezvous.
I say hello to that dear memory.

Between my love and me there's a window.
I gaze out into Spring through the eyes of
someone who loves flowers, whose dreams
are hindered by the little dreams of flowers -
dreams of loss, dreams of goodbye.

Between God and me there's a window
and I have named it Galilee.

John Glenday

إيقاعاتُ الليّل

في الليّلِ تقتربُ
السَّماءُ إلى الذّئابْ
في الليّلِ يتّضحُ السّكونْ
يمشي على سجّادةِ الأفَقِ، التأمّلِ
لا يرى إلّا اتسّاعَ خيالِه
في الليلِ نُصغي لانكسارِ القلبِ
نحزنُ مع يمامِ الرّوحِ
نحضنُ حُلمَنا...
في الليل نقترفُ التذكّرَ والتصوّرَ
نخلطُ الألوانَ معجونًا لأمنيةٍ قديمةْ
في الليل نُبصرُ صوتَنا دونَ القناعْ
الليلُ يصغي للطفولةِ إنْ تَعُدْ،
والحبِّ في شفةِ الحنينْ
الليلُ منبرُ صمتِنا
في الليل تنكسرُ الجهاتْ
في الليل نختصرُ الرحيلَ
إلى مسافاتِ النوافذْ
في الليل ننتظرُ الرُّؤى
في ثوبِ كاهنةِ الضّبابْ
في الليل تتسّـــعُ
التفاصيلُ...المدى...الأسرارُ...
ناحيةُ الغرامْ

الليلُ يكتبُ
دونَ قيدِ
القافيةْ

Rhythms of the Night

At night, the heavens come closer
to wolves.
At night, quiet is transparent,
treads on the carpet of the horizon, of contemplation,
sees nothing but the breadth of its imagination.
At night, we listen to breaking hearts,
we grieve with the spirit's dove,
we embrace our dreams.
At night, we remember and visualise,
mix colours into a paste of old wishes.
At night, we hear our true voice.
Night listens for childhood, in case it returns
and for love on the cusp of desire.
Night is the pulpit of our silence.
At night, directions don't work.
At night, we lessen leaving
to the width of windows.
At night, we wait for dreams, dressed up
as priestesses of fog.
At night, details, distance and secrets encompass
the realm of infatuation.
Night writes
without the restrictions
of rhyme.

Kathrine Sowerby

وحيٌ على سطرِ موجة

الصّيفُ ينفذُ في طباعِ الموجِ
يُلبِسُهُ الوداعةَ،
والجنونُ يوازنُ الإيقاعَ
إنْ تمَّ القمرْ
قيلولةُ الأمواج قبلَ ظهيرةِ الأشواقِ
يكمنُ في خلاياها مهبُّ الملحِ...
تسكنُها جراحُ الحبِّ،
أسرارُ اللّغاتِ
فمــن هنــا مـرّتْ عشــيقـاتُ الأغـاني
من هنا صَعدَ الغريقُ
إلى سماءِ حنينها
أبديّةٌ هيَ لحظةُ الشّمسِ
التي كَشَفَتْ مفاتنَ روحِها
أبديّةٌ هي خطوةُ النّسماتِ
فوقَ شعورِنا العبثيّ
في دربِ الرّمالْ

الكونُ إنسانٌ
يقولُ العارفُ الصّوفيُّ
في لحظاتِ كشفٍ وانبهارْ
وأقولُ: هذا البحرُ دمعةُ عاشقٍ
وسماؤنا الضوءُ المشاكسُ
في عيونِ عشيقةٍ
والغيمُ أحلامُ النهارْ
ونجومُ ليلِ الوجدِ شاماتُ الإلهِ
وظلُّهُ العفويُّ آفاقُ الضحى
والبدرُ دمعُ النّارِ

Inspiration while Watching the Waves

Summer pierces the mood of the waves
it coats them with kindness
when the moon rounds to the full
their rhythm will be partnered by wildness
their midday rest is in the noon of yearning
a breath of salt blown from their hollows…
love's wounds live among them
the secrets of languages
for the women beloved in song have gone by here
and here their drowned lovers have risen
into the sky of their longing
Eternity is the flash of the sun
when it lets you glimpse the power of its beauty
Eternity is when the soul steps
free of our crazy emotions
onto the sand pathway

Says the Sufi master
in a moment of revelation and ecstasy:
the universe is a person
and I say: this sea is from a lover's weeping
and the sky is the quarrelsome light
in the eyes of a beloved
and the clouds are the dreams of daytime
and the stars in nights of love are the birthmarks of Deity
and the horizon at dawn is his passing shadow
and the full moon is the fiery tears

شمعُ الانتظارْ
وأصدّقُ الصوفيّ
والشَّعرَ المرافقَ حُلمهُ
لا بأسَ إنْ آمنتُ
فالحبُّ اتّساعٌ
قال لي صدري
ونبضُ الموجِ ... نبضُ الموجِ ...نبضُ الموجِ... نبضُ ال ...

the candles of one waiting
And I believe the Sufi master
and the poetry of his vision
and it's all right to believe
for love is large enough
said my heart to me
in the beat of the waves… the beat of the waves… the beat of the
waves… the beat   of…

DM Black

عمر شبـانـة

١- الشاعر

مقدّمةٌ:

يقولُ عليه نقادٌ:
قصيدتُهغنائيّةْ
ونقّادٌحدائيون:
رثائيّةْ
ونقّادٌ أشدّ حداثة سيؤكدون:
حديثة لكن.. مباشرةٌ
ونقّادٌ: معلّقةٌ تصوّر ذاتَه
وتقولُ سيرتَه

وفي المقهى
يقولُ شُويعرٌ:
هذي القصيدةُ جِدُّ تافهةٍ،
عموديّةْ

-١-

هنا..
في الطابقِ العاشرْ
يقولُ لروحه الشاعرْ:

بداياتٌ هي الدنيا
نكونُ هُنا

Omar Shabanah
Bridge translation by Jona Fras

The Poet

Introduction:

Here,
critics will say:
his poem is lyrical.
And modernist critics:
elegiac.
And the post-modernists will say:
modernist yet plain.
And some critics will say:
a Mu'allaqa that paints the painter
and tells the poet's story.

And in the coffee shop
a rhymer says:
this poem is a joke...
'conventional!'

1

Here,
on the tenth floor,
the poet tells his soul:

(وأين هنا؟)
ونرحلُ في الـ..هُناكَ

وفي هناك
كأنّما ننسى
وننشغلُ

بداياتٌ تمرّ كما الفُجاءةُ
نحضنُ الأيّامَ.. أحزاناً
وتحضُننا بآلامٍ
ونكتهلُ

بداياتٌ حياةُ الشخص،
رحلتُه،
حدائقُه،
منازلُه الّتي يبني،
خلايا الحبّ في دمِه،
كؤوسُ العُمر يشربُها
على مهَلٍ

بداياتٌ هي.. الأزُلُ

هي الدنيا
تقولُ تعالَ
يا ابن العتمة البيضاء
فالأملُ
يجيءُ كما الحقولُ
كما الينابيعُ

Beginnings are worldly.
We exist here,
and we travel there,
and where is here?

And there
It is as if we forget
or distract ourselves.

Beginnings pass like a shock.
We hold the days with sadness
and they return the embrace with pain
and we grow middle-aged.

The beginnings of a person's life
are their path,
their gardens,
their hand-built homes.
Beads of love in their blood—
measures of life that they drink
slowly.

Beginnings are eternity...

they are earthly.
The world says, come over,
oh son of the white darkness,
and hope
will come too, like the fields,

التي تجري
ولا تصلُ

وبين بدايةٍ وبدايةٍ
نمضي
كأنَّ العمرَ ليلٌ نستريح إليه
من موت طويلٍ

أو عناقٌ عابرٌ
في خلوةٍ للشاعر العابرْ

-٢-

هنا الشاعرْ
سيبدأُ من نهاياتِ الخليقةِ
من عناقِ الدمِّ
من أنثى البداياتِ السحيقةِ
في كتابِ الوَرد
من دمِها الحرائق
من خلايا بحرِها الجبَليٌّ

من جبَلٍ خرافيّ
ومن بحر على الغاباتِ
من شجَرٍ يحدُّ الساحلَ السوريَّ
من إيبلا إلى صيدا
ومن أروادَ
حتّى مركباتِ النارِ
في أثينا

and like the springs
that run
and do not run out.

And between beginnings
we go on,
as if life were a night that rests us
before a long death,

or as if it were a poet's embrace;
fleeting and obscured.

2

Here is the poet.
He will start at the end of creation
from blood's embrace,
from the woman's most distant beginnings
in the book of roses,
from her burning blood,
from the innards of her rising sea.

From a fabled mountain
and from a sea upon the forests.
From the trees that cling to the Syrian coast
from Ebla to Sidon,
and from Arwad
as far as the carriages of fire
in Athens.

هنا الشاعرْ

يُطلُّ من الخليجِ
على نهاياتِ الخليقةِ
أو
يُطلُّ على خرائبِ عُمرِهِ
وعلى جبالِ النحلِ
في أغوارِهِ

ويُطلُّ من عليائِه
فيَرى
هنا..
صندوقَه الأسودْ
هنا أسرارُه
وفضائحُ العتماتِ
تتبعُه
وتسرق ظله
وهنا..

هنا أحلامُه
ورقٌ على ريحٍ
بلا طائرْ

-٣-

هنا..
في الطابقِ العاشرْ
هنا..
في غُرفةٍ..

Here is the poet.

He looks out from the Gulf
upon the ends of creation -
or -
he looks out upon the ruins of his life
and upon the swarm of bees
in his depths.

And he looks out from his heights,
and so he sees

here
his black box.
Here are his secrets
and the degradations of the darkness.
They follow him
and steal his shadow.
And here—

here are his dreams,
a leaf in a wind
without birds.

3

Here
on the tenth floor.
Here

في الطابقِ العاشرْ

هنا..
فوقَ المدينةِ
بين أبراج المدينة
فوقَ بحرٍ هادئٍ
بين ارتعاشاتٍ وضَوءٍ ساخنٍ
بين انكساراتٍ وحلْمٍ
يرقدُ الطائرْ

هنا
في ليلِهِ
في الطابقِ العاشرْ
ينامُ الذئبُ مكتهلاً
ينامُ الكهلُ ذئْبيّاً
ينادمُ ليلَ غُربتِه
ويشربُ كأس منفاه
ويرسمُ من مدينتِه
شظايا ذكرياتٍ
أو ظلاماً ساطعاً يكتظُّ بالشُهداءْ

ويعزف في ليالي الموتِ
أغنيةً عن الحرية البيضاءْ

ويكتب من مدينة عشقه حباً
يغني حالماً بمدينة الأحلام
يقرأ ذكرياتٍ تشرّدٍ
ويطير مختنقاً بوهم الموت..
....

in a room
on the tenth floor.

Here
above the city,
among the towers of the city
above a quiet sea,
among tremors and warm light.
among fractures and a dream,
a bird lies down to rest.

Here
in his night
on the tenth floor
the aging wolf sleeps.

But the old man is still wolflike,
having drinks with the night of his exile,
and he drinks to the tune of those banished from the cup
and he sketches all over his city
scraps of memory,
and a shining darkness filled with martyrs.

And he plays, in death's nighttime,
a song about candid freedom.

And he writes love from the city of his passion.
He sings, dreaming of the city of his visions.
He reads memories of wandering

....

كهلٌ
يحاولُ أن يُعيدَ طفولةً
ويعيدَ أشجاراً
وحقلاً كانَ يلسعُه بشمسِ الغَورِ

كهلٌ يستعيدُ بيادرَ انتُهكتْ
على إيقاعِ بحرٍ ميّتٍ
وصدى فدائيّينَ عندَ النهرِ

كهلٌ ناهَزَ الخمسينَ

كهلٌ لا يحسُّ كهولةً في الروحِ
بل في الذكرياتِ
كهولةٌ تنمو كما الشجَرُ

هنا
في الطابقِ العاشرْ
تجيءُ الذكرياتُ
كما يجيءُ الوحش
في الغربة

هنا
في الطابقِ العاشرْ
هنا طفلٌ يخبِّئُ في حقيبتِه
دفاترَ من رصاصٍ للفدائيّينْ

فتىً حمَلَ الرسائلَ

and flits about, choking on the illusion of death.

An old man
tries to bring back childhood,
and bring back trees,
and a field that stings him with the heat of the Jordan Valley.

A grown man bringing back threshing floors that were broken
to the rhythm of a dead sea
and the sound of the fedayeen by the river.

A grown man pushing fifty.

A grown man who does not feel middle-aged in spirit,
but in memories
his middle age grows like a tree.

Here,
on the tenth floor,
memories come
like the beast that follows exile.

Here
on the tenth floor.
Here, there is a child who hides jotters
made with fedayeen bullets
in his bag.

A boy who took messages

من مخيِّمه إلى منفى المكاتبِ
حالِماً بهواءِ قريتِه وراءَ النهرِ
يتبعُ نهرَ أفكارٍ
ويسبحُ في مياهِ العزلةِ السوداءْ

هنا رجُلٌ
تشرَّدَ في العواصمِ
حاملاً وهماً جميلاً
في حقائبه اسمه: الثورة

وضلَّ وضاعَ
ضاعَ وضلَّ
حتَّى ضاقت الدنيا بقامتِه
وصارَ فضاؤه.. حُفرة

هنا
في الطابقِ العاشرْ

هنا تتجمّعُ السنَواتُ يوميّاً
هنا كهلٌ
يجمّعُ ذكرياتِ العُمرِ
جدّاتٍ وأحفاداً
يَرى ما لا يرى الناسُ

يَرى في عُمرِه برقاً عجوزاً
قادماً من عهدِ آدمَ
أو
يَرى السنواتِ أيّاماً

from his camp to his exile in the office towers.
Dreaming of the air in his village behind the river
he follows a river of thoughts
and plunges into black wells of isolation.

Here is a man
who has wandered through the capitals
hiding a beautiful illusion in his bags:
a picture called the revolution.

And he was misled and mislaid.
Mislaid and misled
until he lost himself in the world
and his universe became a pit.

Here,
on the tenth floor.

Here the years gather, day by day.
Here, a grown man
picks up the memories of life,
gathers grandmothers and children,
and sees what people do not see.

He sees, in his age, a decrepit spark
coming from the age of Adam -
or -
he sees the years as days.
Here, a grown man.

هناكهلٌ
هنا..
في المنزلِ الملمومِ
في (ماركو)
قُرَيْبَ بحيرةٍ صُغرى

هنا..
ما بين فيروزٍ وكورساكوفَ
بين البحر والجبلِ

وبين حضارةٍ دالثْ
وبين حضارةٍ همجيّةٍ
تحتلُّ صدرَ الكَونِ
بين الصينِ والرومانِ والهكسوسِ..
يأتي الراحلون إليهِ
يَحضُرُ كلُّ عشّاقِ الزمانِ هنا

ويحضر طرْفُةُ بنُ العبدِ
مصطحباً جحيمَيْنِ

هنا أوفيد مصطحباً كتاب «المسخْ»
هنا دانتي بكوميديا الإله.. يصوغ رحلته

هنا روح ابن برد والمعرّي
والنواسيّون
والغجرُ البدائيونْ

هنا دالي وبيكاسو وجرنيكا
ولوركا جاء يحمل سِفرَ نيرودا

Here,
brought together in the house ,
in the poet's House
near to a pool.

Here
whatever's between Fayrouz and Korsakov,
between the sea and the mountains,

and between a civilization whose turn has come
and between an earlier civilization
that occupies the heart
between the Chinese and the Romans and the Hyksos.
The departed are drawn to him,
here
all the lovers of time are present.

And Tarfa ibn al-Abd has arrived
with a choice of two hells.

Here is Ovid with his Metamorphoses.
Here is Dante with the Divine Comedy, forging his journey.

Here is the spirit of Ibn Burd and al-Ma'arri,
and those followers of Abu Nuwas,
and the savage drifters.

Here is Dali and Picasso and Guernica,
and Lorca came carrying Neruda's text

ليشهد أنه قد عاش..
كافاقي ليكتب لوحة المدن الخراب

هنا..

هنا أنا
صورة أخرى من «الأرض اليباب»
هنا إيكو.. الذي
رسم الكنيسة باسم وردته
وهنري في «مدارات» الفضيحة
والتّ ويتمانْ حاملاً أوراق عشب يابسٍ يبكي

هنا السيّابُ
يحكي قصة عن مومس عمياء
يعرفها
ويبكي غربة فوق الخليج
هنا
هنا في الطابق العاشرْ

أتى الجنديُّ والعدوانْ
أتى عمرانُ
من ملاّجة الشعراءْ

وجاء محمد القيسيّ
يقرأ في الوداعيّة:
«لأيّامي
لدفقة زعتر الجبلِ»
أتى من مهرجان جرشْ
ليبكي مقتل الحنّونْ

to show that he had lived,
and here is Cavafy to write a sign for ruined cities.

Here.

Here I am
another image from The Waste Land.
Here is Eco, who
drew the church with the name of the rose
and Henry in the Tropic of scandal.
Walt Whitman crying with his dry leaves of grass.

Here is Al-Sayyab,
telling a story about a blind prostitute.
He knows her
and he pours out his exile across the Gulf.
Here.
Here, on the tenth floor

al-Jundi and 'Adwan came.
Umran came
from Mallaja of the poets
and Muhammad al-Qaysi came.
He came reading The Farewell:
"To my days
To the burst of mountain thyme."
He came from Jerash Festival,
to cry for the killing that grew anemones.
He came from his death

أتى من موته
ليقول غربته
أتى ليقول:
(كم سنموت كي نبقى معاً)
وأتى
ليعزف ناييَ أيام المخيم
أو ليعزف نايه في شارع المنفى

هنا سيبوح صوت الشعر والشاعر:

لروحك يا محمد
يا صديق الصعلكات
وسيد الغزلِ
أعبّ الكأس تلو الكأس
أشرب ما تبقى منك في روحي
وأسكر من قصائدك التي حفرت
دروباً ليس ينساها الزمانُ
أعبّ أياماً شربناها معاً
في المكتب السريّ
أو في بيت ليلى
يا أمير الشعر والترحال..

وجهك لا يفارقني
بلحيتك المهيبةِ
أو بصوتك
ذلك الجبليّ
أو بحدادك الأزليّ
فاذهب في الخلود
إلى نهايات الخلود

to tell of his exile.
He came to say:
"How many times will we die not to part?"
And he came
to play the flute for the days in the camp,
to play his flute in the streets of his exile.

Here, he will let out the sound of poetry and the poet:

To your soul, O Muhammad al-Qaysi,
O friend of the down-and-out
and master of ghazals,
I gulp glass after glass.
I drink whatever remains of you in myself,
and I get drunk on your poems which carved
tracks that time does not forget.
I slug whole days we drank down together
in the secret office,
or in Layla's house.
O prince of poetry and journeys

your face does not depart
with your solemn beard
or with your voice -
that mountain's voice -
or with your endless mourning.
So I go to eternity.
To the ends of eternity
so, let my blood cry.

ودعْ دمي يبكي
هنا في الطابق العاشرْ

بكى الكهلُ الوحيدُ رفاقَه المتشردين
بكى شعوباًكالهنود الحمر..
ما بادت
ولكن.. أين موسيقا الهنود الحمر
أين غناؤهم ؟

ويكى
بكى شمساً يغطيها غرابٌ معدنيٌّ قادمٌ
من غرب هذا الكون
من تجّار أسلحة وأفيونٍ

بكى قمراً صديقاً غاب في الحاناتِ
يشرب بالكؤوس «مجرةَ القتلى»
وآخرَ مزّقته قذيفة
والثالث اخترقت خلايا روحه
دبّابة السرطانْ

أتى العشب الفلسطينيّ
من دير الغصون
إلى قطنّة في جبال القدسْ

أتى الولد المقمّى بالرماةِ
أتى

أتى ابن مخيم الوحدات
وابن مخيم البقعة

Here, on the tenth floor

the old man cried alone for his wandering friends.
He cried for peoples like the Iroquois,
who were destroyed.
But where is the music of those first nations -
where is their singing?

And he cried.
He cried over a sun blacked-out by metal hawks advancing
from the west of this existence,
from merchants of weapons and morphine.

He cried over a friendly moon that disappeared into the bars,
drinking 'The Galaxy of the Dead' by the glassfull,
and he cried over another moon torn apart by a bomb,
and a third, the cells of whose soul were pierced
by the tracks of cancer.

The Palestinian grass came
from the town of Deir al-Ghusun
to Qatanna in the hills around Jerusalem.

The boy followed by snipers came.
He came,

a child of Wihdat Camp came,
and a child of Baq'a Camp,
here, they met.

هنا اجتمعوا

هنا
في الطابق العاشرْ

هنا..
جلستْ على الكرسيّ أعوامُ الكهولةِ
تشربُ الويسكي
وتبكي
تشربُ الفودكا
وتحكي ذكريات العمرِ..
تنسج ذكريات للغد المقتول والقاتلْ

هنا
في الطابق العاشر
جلستُ أنا

أنا الشاعرْ

أنا في الطابق العاشرْ

أنا الفجأةْ

أنا الطير الذي سرى
من الطوفان آخرَه
ويأتي حاملاً غصن الخلاصِ
هنا..

Here,
on the tenth floor.
Here,
on the seat of middle age,
drinking whisky
and crying,
drinking vodka
and telling the memories of the years,
weaving memories for the murdered and the murdering Tomorrow.

Here
on the tenth floor
I sit.

I am the poet.

I am on the tenth floor.

I am the surprise.

I am the bird that will see
the end of the flood
and come carrying the branch of liberation.
Here.

Here
above the city,
among the towers of the city,

هنا
فوق المدينة
بين أبراج المدينة
لا أرى طفلاً ولا كهلاً

أرى شبحاً نحيلاً غائر العينين مثلي
يشرب الفودكا
وتأمرني أصابعه
فأجلس حيث يجلس
أشرب الفودكا

ونهبط
لست أدري أين
لكني أراني في مرايا روحه
وأراه في روحي

أراه يسير في طرق
يراني وهو ينظر خلفه ليرى طريقي
ثم ضعتُ وضاعْ

أنادي: أنت نوح العصرِ
يصرخ: أنت نوح العصرِ

أصرخ: أنت ميلادي
فيصرخ: أنت موتي
ثم نصرخ:
أنت ميلادي وموتي
يا أخي في الطابق العاشرْ

I do not see a child nor a grown man

I see a thin ghost with sunken eyes like me,
drinking vodka,
his fingers beckoning me,
and I am sitting where he is sitting,
drinking vodka.

And we come down -
I do not know where to
but I see myself in the mirrors of his soul
and I see him in my soul.

I see him walking roads.
He sees me, looking past him to see where I'm going,
then I was lost, and he was lost.

I call out: You are Noah for our age
he shouts: You are Noah for our age

I shout: you are my birth
and he shouts: you are my death
Then we shout:
you are my birth and my death
oh my brother on the tenth floor.

Henry Bell

عبدالله أبو بكر

فلامنكو

مع رقصة الفلامنكو ..
كانت أقدامُ الراقصةِ تُغني ..
وتُرقِّصُ جوفَ الأرض
كان المطربُ
يصرخ بالإسبانيةِ
لن يقتلوني .. لن يقتلوني
تلكَ الرقصةُ كانت حَرباً
ومئاتُ الموجودينَ بقلب المسرحِ
كانوا القتلى!

Abdallah Abu Bakr
Bridge translations by Lloyd Randle

Flamenco

Deep in the heart of the dance
the dancer's feet began to sing
and she made that whole nation
with its empty heart dance with her.

The singer was calling out in Spanish
'They can never kill me! They can never kill me!'
The dance was really a battle, you see;
hundreds of folk in that theatre were killed.

John Glenday

لعيونها

إلى فتاة دمشق

لعيونها ..
أرمي بكلّ ملامحي في النهرِ
أقطفُ من كلامِ الشمسِ
ما يهبُ العبارةَ كلّ هذا الضّوءْ
وأجمعُ ما تناثرَ من أصابعيَ الكثيرةِ
في إناءِ العزفِ
أحمل في يديّ الرملَ إن سارثْ عليهِ
وأشتهي فيهِ الوضوءْ

صلاة حيفا

من حيفا..
كنتُ أسافرُ حتى ... حيفا
فأنا..
مُذ جئتُ صَغيراً
كنتُ تَصافحتُ مع البحرِ على شاطئِها
ورَميتُ بَقلبي في حُفرةِ طينٍ ..
ككيف أصلّي للّه ..
وأعبَدها!

For Her Eyes

To the young woman from Damascus:
For your eyes
I chuck all my dreams in the river
I tear down speech from the sun
All the phrases of light it gives
I take back my fingers that boiled over the oud
Like vegetables in a pot
In my hand I hold the sand she walked on
And my longing to be made pure.

Henry King

A Haifa Prayer

I was on my way from Haifa to Haifa.
That's been my only road ever since I was a child.
I went down to the shoreline and paddled in the ocean
then dug a hole in the sand and buried my heart.
That way I knew for sure I would never forget her.
I gathered up Haifa sand and cleansed myself with it
because, God knows, I know precisely
how I should pray to God
and how I should worship her -
my Haifa.

John Glenday

في الصورة

في الصورةِ
كان رآني
حدّق في وجهِ المرآة ي أبني ذكرايَ بها
كنت توضّأتُ بحبّاتِ الرّملِ
لأعرفَ ..

تلفّت
ورأى جسداً يتساقط
ذاكرةً ملآى بغبارٍ أسود يتزاحم كجراد
عينينِ بلا بصرٍ
وفماً يتعثّرُ بالهمسْ
«هل هذا الذائبُ فيه أنا»
قالَ ..
وقد حاصرهُ البردُ
وذابت في كفّيه الشمسْ

Reflection

He had noticed someone gazing
at him from the reflection.

So he stared back into the mirror's face
then glanced quickly round and saw a body

falling; someone remembered, coated
in black dust that gleamed like locusts

and he saw eyes that couldn't see
and a mouth struggling to speak.

"Is this me dissolving?" he asked
"Is that shapeless puddle really me?"

And the glaciers shouldered in around him
and the sun melted away to nothing in his hands.

John Glenday

عبـد الناصر صالح

امـرأة في الحديقـة

ثَمَّةَ امرأةٌ في الحديقةِ
ثَمَّةَ وَجْهٌ جَميلٌ كشَمْسِ الصّباحِ
وعَيْنانِ تَنْتَسِبانِ للبحرِ،
غادَرَ سِرْبُ العَصافيرِ
وَهيَ جالِسَةٌ حولَ نافورةِ الماءِ ،
(تُشْعِلُ سيجارةً)
تَتأَمّلُ غُصْناً من النّورِ
بينَ خلايا الشَّجَرْ.
- كنتُ أَرْقُبُها -
وهي تُضْفي على الوردِ
رائحةً من شَذاها
ونُحرّرُ ضحكَتَها من إسارِ الضَّجَرْ .

*

ثمةَ امرأةٌ
- كنتُ أَرْقُبُها -
تتأَمّلُ خاتَمَها الذّهَبي
وتقرأُ في سِفرِها قصصَ العشقِ
تَضْحكُ للطيرِ حينَ يُظلّلُها بجَناحيْهِ
ترسمُ في صفحةِ العُشْبِ تُفّاحةً وقَمَرْ.

*

ثَمَّةَ امرأةٌ ،
تَبوّأُ مَقعَدَها الخَشَبيّ
وتَمْشطُ أهدابَها في المرايا
- ما الذي يَتَراءى لها في الحديقةِ ؟

Abdel Nasser Saleh
Bridge translations by Lloyd Randle

Woman in a Landscape

There! A woman in the garden
Look! A face as beautiful as the dawn
and eyes that are descendants of the sea

She sits beside a fountain
a flock of birds takes flight
she smokes a cigarette

watches the light shine
between trees
watched by me

as she wraps a rose
in her own perfume
and laughs

freeing me
from sorrow's prison

There! A woman
watched by me
examining her gold ring

as she reads

قلتُ أُحِبَّ الخُطى نَحْوَها
وتَقَدَّمْتُ ،
لكنّي عُجْتُ مُنكَسِراً مثل غَيْمةِ صَيْفٍ
وتَمَلَّكَني الخَوْفُ
حينَ سَمِعتُ صدى الصّوتِ يأتي
ورَأيْتُهُما ..

....

....

كانتِ الشَّمْسُ تَرْسو بعينيها
وتَوَارَتْ في الظِّلّ.

with a knowing look
love stories in her holy book

laughing
at a bird who tries
to cast a shadow on her

its wings drawing
an apple, a moon
upon the leaves

There! A woman
making a throne
of a wooden bench
as she combs her eyelashes
in the mirror

What is it she sees? I ask
as I rush to be part of her view

But I dissolve like a summer cloud
As I hear a voice approach
and fear is my new prison
as I see them both

The dawn that was anchored
in her eyes, departed
replaced by night

Ellen McAteer

Abdel Nasser Saleh

Woman in a Garden

Look at the woman sitting on the lawn,
and look: her face is beautiful as the dawn,
with eyes that shine like daughters of the ocean.
While she is sitting there beside the fountain,
smoking a cigarette, two doves take flight,
and she contemplates the way a beam of light
dances among the leaves high in a tree.
I watch without her seeing me,
and as she enfolds a flower in her scent
her laughter frees me from sorrow's imprisonment.

§

Look at the woman I am watching
as she sits scrutinising a gold ring;
in the book open on her lap, she reads
stories of passion, and when a bird shades
her with its wings, she laughs, drawing on
a bush's leaves an apple and a moon.

§

Look at the woman who sits on a wooden chair
as if it were a throne; and as she combs her hair
admiring her own elegance in a mirror,
who is it that now stands before her
in the garden? I wondered, as I began to quicken

my steps to show myself.
                        But suddenly stricken,
twisting upon itself like a summer cloud,
my mind became possessed by doubt
when I drew near, and heard the voice of another
and saw them there together...

...

...

The sun, I saw, was setting in her eyes
and darkness, in its place, was on the rise.

Henry King

ماجد أبو غوش

عَـوْدَة

كانت المَرأةُ تَجُرُّ قَدَمَيْها
وَما تَبَقَّى مِن أطْفالِها
باتِّجاهِ ما تَبَقَّى مِنَ البَيْتِ
بِاتِّجاهِ ما تَبَقَّى
مِنَ البَحْرِ
باتِّجاهِ ما تَبَقَّى
مِنَ القلبِ
باتِّجاهِ ما تَبَقَّى
مِنَ القلب!

رَفَعَت يَدَها بِهُدوءٍ
وَمَسَحَت دَمْعَةً تَدَحْرَجَت عَلى خَدِّها
وَابْتَسَمَت عِندَما اعْتَرَضَت طَريقَها
المُذيعَةُ الجَميلةُ وَسَألَتْها:
إلى أيْنَ تَعودينَ ؟
....
لأُرْوي شَجَرَةَ الياسَمين
حتّى تُظَلِّلَ أسْماءَ الشُّهداء !

رام الله
15/8/2006

Majid Abu Ghoush
Bridge translations by Danielle Linehan Kiedaisch

Returning

the woman was dragging her feet
and what remained of her children
towards what remained of her home
towards what remained
of the sea
towards what remained
of the heart
towards what remained of the heart

she raised her hand softly
wiped a tear which rolled down her cheek
and smiled when the beautiful one
she met on the way asked her:
why are you going back?

to water the jasmine tree
to shade the names of the martyrs

Magi Gibson

عَـوْدَة

كانت المَرأةُ تَجُرُّ قَدَمَيها
وَما تَبَقّى مِن أطْفالِها
باتِّجاهِ ما تَبَقّى مِنَ البَيْتِ
باتِّجاهِ ما تَبَقّى
مِنَ البَحْرِ
باتِّجاهِ ما تَبَقّى
مِنَ القلبِ
باتِّجاهِ ما تَبَقّى
مِنَ القلب!

رَفَعَت يَدَها بِهُدوءٍ
وَمَسَحَت دَمْعَةً تَدَحْرَجَت عَلى خَدِّها
وَابْتَسَمَت عِندَما اعْتَرَضَت طَريقَها
المُذيعَةُ الجَميلةُ وَسَألَتْها:
إلى أيْنَ تَعودينَ ؟
. . . .
لأرْوي شَجَرَةَ الياسَمين
حتّى تُظَلّلَ أسْماءَ الشُّهداء !

رام الله
15/8/2006

tilleadh

bha am boireannach a' slaodadh a casan
is na tha air fhàgail bho a clann
gu na tha air fhàgail bhon taigh
gu na tha air fhàgail
bhon a' mhuir
gu na tha air fhàgail
bhon a' chridhe
gu na tha air fhàgail bhon a' chridhe!

thog i a làmh gu socair
a' suathadh deur a bha sleamhnadh sìos a gruaidhe
dèanamh gàire nuair a choinnichear i air a slighe
dh'fheòraich an t-aithrisear àlainn:
càite bheil thu a' tilleadh

. . . .

a thaiseach na craoibhe seasamain
do fhasgadh nan ainm martaireach!
Ramallah 15/8/2006

Aonghas MacNeacail

البكاءُ على صَدْرِ غَزَّة

ماءُ البحرِ مالحٌ
وَدَمْعُكِ
* * *
نعمْ سَيِّدَتي
هذا الذي على رِدائِكِ
دَمي
* * *
والذي رَفَعَني على الصَّليبِ
كانَ أخي !
والذي دَفَعَني إلى البِئرِ
كانَ أخي

والذي أضْرَمَ النّارَ في الكَرْمِ
وفي القَلْبِ
كانَ أخي
* * *
والذي أطْلَقَ النّارَ
على أُغْنياتِ المَساءِ
كانَ أخي
* * *
والذي أطْلَقَ النّارَ
على وَجْهِ القَمَرِ
كانَ أخي
* * *
والذي ضَغَطَ على الزِّنادِ
وَياسِمِ الرَّبِّ

Crying on Gaza's Chest

Salt sea water
and your tears

Yes, madam
this is my blood
on your clothes

It was my brother
who lifted me
on to the cross
my brother
who pushed me
into the well

My brother
who set fire
to the vineyard
and my heart

My brother
who opened fire
on the evensong

My brother
who opened fire
on the moon's face

Majid Abu Ghoush

أُراقَ عَلى الرَّملِ دَمي
كانَ أخي

My brother
who pulled the trigger
in the name of the Lord
splashing my blood
on the sand

Ellen McAteer

Majid Abu Ghoush

Gal air broilleach gaza

sàl saillte
is do dheòir
***

seadh a bhean uasail
's e tha seo air do ghùn ach
m'fhuil-sa!
***

am fear a thog mi air a' chrois
b'e mo bhràthair!
is a phut mi dhan tobar
b'e mo bhràthair!
***

is a chuir lasair ris an fhionnghart
's ris a' chridhe
b'e mo bhràthair!
***

is a loisg urchair
air na h-òrain feasgair
b'e mo bhràthair!
***

is a loisg urchair
air gnùis na gealaich
b'e mo bhràthair!
***

is a tharraing an t-òrd-ghunna
ann an ainm an tighearna
is a shil m'fhuil air a ghaineamh

b' e mo bhràthair!

Aonghas MacNeacail

احتباسٌ

البحرُ
أظنُّ أنّه أوْسَعُ
وأشدُّ زُرْقَةً
الشَّمسُ
أظنُّ أنّها أجملُ
وأكْثرُ دِفْئاً
الطُّرقاتُ
أظنُّ أنّها أطولُ
وأكثرُ انسياباً
العشقُ
أظنُّ أنّه مؤلمٌ
وأكثرُ من الفراشاتِ
احتراقاً
القمرُ
مثلُ عَيْنَيكِ
ليلٌ وسحرٌ
يدنو من الموتُ اشتياقا
الصُّبحُ
مَلَلُ الليلِ
من قَمَرٍ
أطالَ البُكاءَ والشَّكوى
وغناءَ السّكارى
الشعر
ساحة الغامِ
حد فاصل
بين الموت والحياة
وأغنية تظل تراوح

Detention

In my mind
the sea is wider
bluer

In my mind
the sun is warmer
kinder

In my mind
the roads are longer
they flow like water

In my mind
passion is painful
a bonfire of moths

The moon, like your eyes
(night and magic as they die)
yearns for morning:

a moon weary of night
of too much crying
drunken song and poetry

A theatre of landmines
fencing life from death
the song veering

Majid Abu Ghoush

بين اليقظة والجنون
الكونُ
حيثُ تكونينَ
جاهِرَةً للقِطافِ
وحيثُ أكونْ

رام الله المحتلة
17/11/2006

from relevance to insanity
the Universe
from which

you are ready
to be plucked
as am I

Ellen McAteer

اِحْتِلال

ظلٌّ أسودٌ لِكائِنٍ غَريبٍ
على نافِذَةٍ مُطْفَأَةْ
رائِحَةُ المَوتِ
في ظَهيرةٍ قائِظَةْ
شَيءٌ ثَقيلٌ
يَجثِمُ على الصَّدرِ والجَفْنَيْن
ألمٌّ في الحَلْقِ
وأسفلِ الظَّهرِ

غُبارٌ أسْودٌ
يُغَطّي أوْراقَ الوَرْدِ
حَيثُ يوجدُ
تَلَوُّثٌ بيئيّ
عَرَباتٌ سَوْداءُ
تُرْفَعُ راياتٌ عَلَيْها
عَظْمَتانِ وَجُمْجُمَةْ
مَوتٌ مُبَكِّرٌ
وَكَوابيسُ طَوالَ الوَقتْ
فِرَقُ إعْدامٍ
وَمُعَسكراتُ اعتقالٍ
رَنَّةُ عودٍ
حَزينةٌ
وآثارُ أقْدامِ الغُزاةْ

رام الله المحتلة
17/11/2006

Occupation
Occupied Ramallah 17/11/06

Strange days cast dour shadows.
Dusk. The fragrance of death
on a windowsill.
In the lingering heat
an impossible burden weighs
down on eyelids and chest;
the throat aches, the spine throbs.

Rose petals all tarnished with foul dust
from the poisoned world.
Black limousines sail past, flying
the skull and crossbones.
The grave yawns open early,
nightmares never leave.
Death squads. Detention camps.

Somewhere, an oud
pronounces its sad chords.
The invaders smile; tap their feet.

John Glenday

رانيـة ارشـيد

رقص على صوت عـار

صوتَها
كأنّني غُبَارٌ عَلى مَعَانٍ،
كأنّني انغِلاقُ صَدرٍ حَتى
فُسحة الفراغ.
عُزلَتي، التي لا تَقبَل القِسمَة عَلينَا، تَجعَلُني أُجيدُ
الرَّقص عَلى هوامِش تأتأةِ الكَلام
أو أكثَر

تُوَجِّلني الخُطى بحروفِهَا المُدمَّاة
فنَصمِتُ مَن كَثرَة الكَلامِ ،
وَلا نُدرِكَ لأن لِلبَحرِ لَونَاً لا نَعرِفُهُ.

صَوته
نِداءٌ مِن جَوفِ الكلماتِ، جَسَدٌ تَنسابُ
فِيهِ شَهوَةُ الصَّوت..
هُوَ أنتِ
غَريبةٌ عِندَما تَأخُذِك مِني لُغَتي
فأرتَكِبُ أفحَشَ الأمنيَات
أتَساءَلُ أحيَاناً :
- كيفَ التَّخلصُ مِن غُربةِ الرُّوح ؟

صُورَة
سَريرٌ مُراهِقٌ، وامرَأةٌ بِجَناحٍ كَهِلٍ
تَتكئُ عَلى شُرفَةٍ شاطئ.
تَعُدُّ للوَراءِ الجُروح، تُقدّمُ لَها بَقَايا اعتِذارٍ مِنهَا،

RANIA IRSHAID
Bridge translation by Sarah Irving

Dance on a naked voice

Her voice:

My fears fuzz up the tap
turn it off
my voice will never fill
this space

My loneliness makes me expert
a dancer on the edge of speech
stuttering, holding back
footsteps tattoo a message

talk is silenced
no-one knows it
the sea
is such a strange colour

His voice:

Someone is calling
a body become a running tap
in its desire for sound

It's you
I am a stranger
when my words
take you from me
I commit obscenity
in my desires

قَبلَ انعِطافِ عُمرِها عِندَ الأُفّ

صَوت آخر
هُوَ؛ انعِدامُ خُطى في طريقٍ تَّقفّر
هيَ؛ انسكابُ صِبَا جَاف عَلَى قَارِعَةِ أَرَقٍ
هُما؛ انقِسامُ جَسدٍ في ظِلِ فَراغٍ

نَكادُ نَكونُ؛
ثَمَرَةً مُدلاةً تُرتَعِشُ مِن قِطافٍ مُحرّمٍ
أو رَحيقٍ يَّتَوارى في سَديمِهِ

صدى صَوتِه
صَدى رَطبٌ يَّتَسَلّلُ مِن خُطى مُراوغَة
كُلّما اكتَمَلَت فينا رَقصَةُ فَراشةٍ
يَتَخَثَّرُ الضَّوءُ، فنُسرعُ لِنُلَملِم مَا بَينَنا
مِن عَبَثٍ زَبَد ارتِطامِنَا

أعرفُني أُغمِضُ قَلبي نِصفَ إغماضةٍ
لِيَرى مَا بِدَاخِلِهِ مِن أُخاديدِ شَوقٍ.
هَكذا، يَبدأُ الفَجرُ بِنَزعِ مَخالِبِ لَيلِهِ،
مِن رَمَاد عُشبِ الجسَدِ .

صدى صَوتَه
إنّها الخَطيئةُ؛ لا تَسأل عَن هَندَسَةِ لِشكلِها
أو بَياضِها المَاكِر الذي يَجرَحُ خَدَّ الطُّفولة
إنّها مبضعٌ يَحتالُ على غفلَتي كَي تَّسرّبُ إليَّ مِن حِبرٍ كَسولٍ

تِلكَ هيَ ؛ تَدخُلُ إليَّ مِن جِهَتي الخَامسة
المتآكلة مِن صَلصَالِ فقديدهَا
كَي تَبيحَ سِترَ عُربي

I wonder sometimes
how to reach you

A picture:

A teenager's bed
and a woman on the verge
of old age, leaning over a balcony
by the sea, preparing
from behind the wounds of time
an apology for them
turning back her years

Another voice:

He: the absence of footsteps on the road destroys
She: the spilling of powder in the street is insomnia
They: the division of the body is the shadow of the void

Almost being:

The hanging fruit trembles
from forbidden picking
the nectar melts in the haze
of the flower

His echo:

A damp echo
of retreating footsteps
whenever we flutter
together
for a moment

Light congeals

Rania Irshaid

and we hurry to gather
up what is left to us
of the futile froth
of our collision

I tell myself I am hiding
my half-shadowed heart
to see what kind of thick
longing is within it

And so the night blunts
the dawn's claws
from the ashes
of the body's
vegetation

Her echo:

She is sin, for sure
don't ask how she was made
or about her cunning whiteness
an injury to childhood's cheek

Surely a scalpel has tricked its way
to me from this idle ink

This is she: she enters into me
from my fifth direction
chafed by the powder which conceals
as it permits, my nakedness

Ellen McAteer

يوسف أبو لـوز

خيــــل

ما الدنيا؟
قال الملك المملوك : الدنيا قصري
العاشقُ قال : الدنيا بيتُ حبيبٍ لا تبصره العينُ،
وقال الجندي الخاسر :
الدنيا نعشي.

ما الدنيا؟
قال الموسيقيُّ: الدنيا عودي المشدودُ بخمسِ خصالٍ
من خمسِ نساءْ.
والحوذيّ الأشيبُ حَطَّ أصابعه في الشيبِ،
وقال : الدنيا رأسي
قال الخطّاط: الدنيا مَحْوٌ وكتابة.
والمرأة قالت: ماءْ
الآثمُ قال:
الدنيا اليومَ
لكي أنسى أمسيْ.
وأنا قلت : الدنيا فرسي.
سكّانُ الدنيا ماتوا ...
ذهبوا للمجهولِ،
وما زلتُ أسابق قطعان الرّيحِ،
على فرسي.

Yousef Abu Loz
Bridge translations by Cate Pollock

The Horse Rider

What is the world?
The king of the slaves said: the world is my castle.
The lover said: the world is the house of the beloved, unseen by the eye.
and the lost soldier said:
the world is my coffin.
What is the world?
The musician said: the world is my lute's five strings, each of them a
woman
with a woman's qualities.
And the white-haired driver placed his finger in his hair,
and said: the world is my head.
The calligrapher said: the world is an erasure and an inscription
and the woman said: water
and the sinner said: the world is today
for I have blotted out my yesterdays.
And I said: the world is my horse.
All the people in the world are dead,
passed over to the unknown.

And still I am on my horse,
racing with the flocks of the wind.

Donald Adamson

ثلاثةُ بنّائيـن

بنّاؤونَ ثلاثة
الأولُ كهلْ
الثاني رجلٌ كالسهل
والثالث شابْ
كانوا في حانةٍ «لشبونة» يبنونَ مدينة،
الكهلُ بنى معْبد
الرجل السهل بنى متجرْ
والشاب بنى ملعبْ
في حانةِ لشبونة بنّاءون ثلاثة،
ماتَ الكهلُ على المقعد
نامَ الرجل السهل على خشب المشربِ محفوراً بالليلِ
وما زال الشابُّ،
على ملعبه ... يلعبْ.

ثلاثة أسـلاف

نحنُ ثلاثةُ أسلافٍ،
من قدماءِ الإغريقِ،
ذبحنا عِجْلَ الأيتامِ،
وأطفأنا نارَ السَّحَرةْ.
أنا،
والحطّابُ الكهلُ،
وأُختي الشَّجَرة ..

Three Builders

Three builders
The first middle aged
The second a man like smooth ground
And the third a young man
Built a city in the 'Lisbon' bar.
The middle-aged man built a temple
The smooth man built a shop
And the young man built a playing field.
In the Lisbon bar were three builders
The middle-aged man died where he sat
The smooth man slept alone on the bar that night
But the young man didn't stop –
On his field, he keeps playing…

Henry King

Three Ancestors

We are three ancestors
From the times of the ancient Greeks,
We killed the orphaned calf,
And put out the sorcerers' fire.
Me,
The middle-aged wood-gatherer,
And my sister the tree.

Henry King

آخـر القـرن

كلّما أتقدّمُ في العمرِ،
أعرفُ أنَّ بلادي أمامي
فأحثُّ أمتعتي لأطيرَ إليها
وأنظرُ خلفي لئلا يكونَ الغزاةُ ورائي
أتلّفتُ ثانيةً : وأحثُّ الخُطى ... صائحاً:
يا بلادي انطريني ...
إنني الآنَ في آخرِ القرنِ،
ما زلتُ أركُضُ
والعمرُ يركضُ بي
والغزاةُ ورائي
ولكنّهم سَبقوني إليها.
كلّما أتقدمُ في العمرِ،
أعرفُ أن حياتي ورائي
فأبكي عليها.

Last of the Century

Knowing my country is far
I pack my cases and fly
always checking over my shoulder
to see if I am shadowed, always
looking around: paranoid

I hasten my wings, oh
wait for me, my country, I am lost
in the century. I swoon and swoop
with the invaders' hot breath
on my neck and even though
I rush past a decade of years
they still beat me to her.

I've become older, I know my life
is behind me. Where I cannot fly.

Ryan Van Winkle

سميح محسن

طنين

على قدمي تَعْبرُ الريح،
تمرُّ السواقي
ونحلَةُ رأسي مطوقة بالرذاذ الطريّ
وبالنار والموج.
أمدُّ يديَّ وأفصلُ رأسي
أدحرجه فوق طاولة الأبنوس.
أمدُّ يديَّ وأفتحُ رأسي
وأنزعُ منه الفتيلْ
ولكنَّ نحلة رأسي تطنُّ

تطنُّ

تطنُّ

تطنُّ.

Samih Mohsen
Bridge translations by Aidan Donovan

Buzzin

A wind rolls acroass ma feet
the river keeps runnin
Thurs a bee in ma heed
driven daft wae drizzle an fire an waves
So a whip oot a knife an cut off ma heed
lit it roll err the table
A lift up ma hammer an smash the scalp
tae rip oot its wick
but the bee in that heed

    is buzzin

      still buzzin

        still buzzin

William Letford

تكوين

على حافة النهرِ
شَرقيّ عَدْنٍ
توَقف
حيثُ بنى اللهُ جنتهُ قربَ جيحون.
ثمَّ انحنى كي يغبَّ من الماء.
رأى ظِلّهُ
- عارياً كان مثلَ الظمأ -
تَفَحّصَ ذاتيه:
تلك التي بين عُشبِ البراري
وتلك التي فوق ماءٍ تموجُ
أصيب بنار الذهولِ
وقال : أرى فيّ ما ليس فيّ!
على حافة النهرِ
عاريةً وقفتْ
وانحنتْ كي تَغُبّ من الماء،
رأت ظِلّها
تفحصتْ الظل والذات
قالت : أرى فيّ ما ليس فيّ!
على حافة النهر
من غير أن يشربا الماء
همّا ينامان كلٌّ على ظله
ليطابق ذاتيهِ فالتصق الجسدان
وصرنا.

Creation

At the edge of the river
East of Eden
He paused on his way
Where God had made Paradise beside the River Gihon.
As he bent down to gulp at the water
He saw his shadow
– Nakedness was like thirst –
And inspected himself:
Who lies among wild grasses
Who bends over rippling water
He burned with amazement
And said: I see in myself what is not there!

At the edge of the river
She stood naked
As she bent down to gulp at the water
She saw her shadow
She inspected her shadow and herself
And said: I see in me what is not there!

At the edge of the river
Despite drinking the water
They sleep on their separate shadows
Which cling, identical, to their two bodies
Thus were we created.

Henry King

هراء

يحطُّ على رأسي الطيرُ
ينقرُ جُمجُمتي مثلما ينقُر الخشبَ اليابس
وفي مركز المخ يَعْلقُ منقارُهُ
ويفتشُ عن صفحةٍ في العراءْ
- هكذا خيّلَ الأمرُ لي ، في البداية -
ولكنه عاد ينقرُ مخّي
ليصنع مائدة من خواء
هراءْ ...

Haivers

The burd lichts on ma pow
It howks oot ma heid like it wis dry widd
And at the hert o ma harns its neb steiks
Rakin aboot for a blaud ootby –
I jalouse that's hoo it wis at the stert –
But it gaed back syne tae howkin oot ma heid
Tae mak a kist fou o naethin
Haivers…

James Robertson

Nonsense

A bird landed on my head
It hollowed out my skull as if it were made of wood
And got its beak stuck in the cleft of my brain
It's looking for a fold on the outside
– So I thought to begin with –
But it went back to carving out my head
To fashion a box full of emptiness
Nonsense…

Henry King

نحيب

في ساحة المهدِ
- وقتَ الظهيرة -
كانتْ مقاعِدُ مقهى الرصيف
تعبئها سائحاتٌ أتينَ من الغربِ في شهر أيلولَ
يشْرَبْنَ ماءَ الحنينِ إلى الله.
وكانت تعجُّ الشوارعُ بالعابرين
اللغاتِ الغريبةِ
عبرنا على ظلٍّ
كهلٍ تمطَّى الرصيف بدون انتباه
توَسَّدَ ساعده والحذاء الممزقَ
نامَ على قصة ما ...
نمرُّ على جرحه لا نراه
تدغدغ أجسادَنا الجعةُ ، القهقهاتُ
الحكاياتُ من غير معنى
نحاول أن نُخرجَ الطفلَ في ذاتنا
نعتلي ساحة المهدِ
نرقصُ رقصة زوربا الأثيني
نضحكُ
وندخلُ
ندخلُ في حلقة للنحيبْ.

Lamentation

In Manger Square, at midday,
The chairs outside the cafés
Are taken by Western tourists, in September
They sip at their longing for God
The streets teem with passers-by
And foreign languages
We tread on the shadow
Of an old man stretched out on the pavement
With his arm and a tattered shoe for a pillow
His mattress was a story…
We pass by his wounds without seeing
Beer tickles our bellies to laughter
And telling inane anecdotes
We try to release the child inside us
We stand in Manger Square
And mimic the dance-steps of Zorba the Greek
We step
We laugh
We step into the ring of lamentation.

Henry King

Samih Mohsen

نحيب

في ساحة المهدِ
- وقتَ الظهيرة -
كانتْ مقاعدُ مقهى الرصيف
تعبّئها سائحاتٌ أتينَ من الغربِ في شهر أيلولَ
يشْرَبْنَ ماءَ الحنينِ إلى الله.
وكانت تعجُّ الشوارعُ بالعابرين
اللغاتِ الغريبةِ
عبرنا على ظلٍّ
كهلٍ تمطّى الرصيف بدون انتباه
توَسَّدَ ساعده والحذاء الممزقَ
نام على قصة ما ...
نمرُّ على جرحه لا نراه
تدغدغ أجسادَنا الجعةُ ، القهقهاتُ
الحكاياتُ من غير معنى
نحاول أن نُخرجَ الطفلَ في ذاتنا
نعتلي ساحة المهدِ
نرقصُ رقصة زوربا الأُيني
نضحكُ
وندخلُ
ندخلُ في حلقة للنحيبْ.

An caoineadh

Ann an Ceàrnag Breith Chrìosd
  aig meadhan latha san t Sultain
Suidheachain taobh a-muigh nan cafaidhean
Làn mhnathan-turais bhon Iar
Iad ag òl uisge's a' sireadh Dhè
Othail nan sràidean
Cànain choimheach
Thog sinn oirnn dhan dubhar,
Bodach na shìneadh air a' chabhsair gun diù dha
A ghàirdean agus seann bhròg mar chluasaig
Chaidil e air an naidheachd
Thèid sinn seachad air fhèin's air a lotan gun fhaicinn.
Leann nar stamaig, lachan gàire
Sgeulachdan gun seadh.
A' feuchainn air làithean ar n-òige fhaighinn uair eile,
Seasaidh sinn ann an Ceàrnag Breith Chrìosd
Dannsaidh sinn an danns aig Sòrba na h-Àithne
Togaidh sinn oirnn gàire
Togaidh sinn oirnn a-steach.
A-steach do chearcall a' chaoinidh

Gillebride MacMillan

خيبة

على باب غرفتها
في «الموتيل» المطلّ على البحرْ،
وقفتُ
تذكرتُ ضحكتَها في الممر
وكانت تعودُ الظهيرة مُبتلةً بالعرقْ.
تذكرتُ إيماءةَ العينِ
يديها تعيدان للشعرِ جمرتَه
خفةَ الظلّ،
بنفسجةٌ في يديّ
وقول سأنشده بالأهازيجْ.
نَقرتْ خفيفاً إيصبعي المنحني
أطلت عليّ
على بابِ غرفتها تأتأ القلبُ
أغلقتُ البابَ
أغلقتُ قلبي بقفلٍ صدئ.

Disappointment

At the door to her room
In the motel looking over the sea
I stood
Thinking of how she laughed in the corridor
When she came back that afternoon, damp with sweat.

I remember the look she gave me
Hands that made her hair flash
So lissom
A violet I held
And a song I will sing.

She prised me open with two crooked fingers
She looked at me
At the door to her room the heart stammers
She bolted the door
I bolted shut my heart with a rusty padlock.

Henry King

القميص

علّقتُ قميصي الداكنَ فوقَ المشجَبْ.
وجلستُ على كرسيٍّ خشبيٍّ في زاوية الغرفةِ
أقرأُ ذاتي
أتهجّى بقعَ الملحِ
مرايا التعب النازِف تحتَ الإبطينِ
يُعرّفَني القريون بلونِ قميصي
كنتَ نرجسةً في عمري
أول قيدٍ أكسره الليلة
كي تعبرَ نسماتُ البحرِ الغريبةُ جسدي
وتطهره من دبقِ لُزوجته
من رملِ الصحراءِ / غبارِ الجديلةِ / رائحةِ الروثِ / تقارير الاستخبارات / ورائحة التبغ المسورد
تمحو آثار أصابع امرأة صفعتني لمّا صبّحت عليها في السوق ومني...
أخلع عني الليلةَ هذا الأرثَّ
أُعلقُهُ كالذّبح
وأطلقُ جلدي للريح
أحاول أن أخلد للنّ و مْ.
أتقلّب فوقَ بلاط الغرفةِ
أنسج لي جلداً آخر يحميني من بردِ الفجر
القلق الطارد للنومِ
أحاوِلُ...
أفشلُ

أتغطى بقميصي
فأنامْ.

The Shirt

I hung my dark shirt on the clothes-hook
And sat in a wooden chair in the corner
Now I read myself
I spell out the salt-stains
Mirrors of fatigue dripping from my armpits
The Qariun neighbourhood teaches me what colour my shirt is
You were a daffodil that bloomed in my life
A shackle I break for the first time tonight
As sea-breezes cross my body
And cleanse it of stickiness
Cleanse it of desert sand/dust and matted hair/the smell of dung/
intelligence reports/the scent of imported tobacco
And the finger-marks of the woman who slapped me in the market
Tonight I pull off this inheritance
I hang it up as if for the slaughter
My skin freed to the wind
I try to fall asleep
I writhe about on the tiles
I weave myself another skin to shield me from the cold of dawn
Anxiety knocks like a bailiff in my sleep
I try…
I give up
My shirt covers me
And I sleep.

Henry King

فيصل قرقطي

مختارات من ديوان: " بيت في وشم الخريف"

ينثرُ الغيمُ
أهدابَهُ
في دماءِ الوصيّةِ
وللنهارِ
متعةُ التقصِّي الحالمُ
بوردةِ الحياةْ.

*

جَدّي الماءُ
وأُمّي بتلةُ ضوءٍ في عينيكِ
وأنا ماءُ الأحفادِ بجرْحِ الشعراءْ.
يتنفَّسُني غضبُ الكوْنِ ، ويشرقُ بي مطرُ الغيْمِ ، فَمَنْ دلَّ الصحراءَ عليَّ ؟! وأستبطئُ أشباحي
في الريحِ ، يَقيمونَ صلاةَ الفجْرِ ، وينتذرونَ لترتيلةِ تأبين الجسدِ، يقومونَ على تعبٍ من ماءٍ
ودماءٍ ليعودوا في موتٍ من ماءٍ ودماءٍ تزْهِرُ فيها أحلااااامُ الأرْضِ ، تتفتَّحُ منها أشرعةٌ ، لا تقفُ
على حدِّ الشفقِ ، تضيعُ مع الأيامِ؛ وتكتملُ الصورةُ في ذوبانِ وجودي ، تحتَ سنابكِ خيْلِ
الحلمِ .. لأعرفَ ماهيّةِ كوْنٍ يطبعني بخيوطِ الأرْضِ ، ويكتبني ضوءاً في بستانِ عيونكِ /

*

وأنا
من شطآنٍ منسية
نضَّدْتُ حروفي
وطلعتُ إلى الوقتِ بكلِّ عرائي
وسلاحي الصبرُ المأزومُ على علّاتِ
اللغة
أتمنْطقُ باليأسِ
خذيني للخذلانِ يخرُّ على
صدْري الكهّانُ / يرونَ براعتَهم في

Faisal al-Qarqati
Bridge translations by Telche Hanley-Moyle

An excerpt from haudin the kenmark o hairst

cloods hale
thair ruinds
throu tim-telt bluid
    n day breks
    the wunner o warkin tae the ruit n the rise
    o the leevin rose.

*

    ma grandfaither   the watter
    n ma mither   a petal of licht i yer een
    n A the watter-bairn   fae a poet's skaith.

A'm the braith o wraith, clood-tuimin wraith, sae wha's this desert fer?
n A'm bidin yet fer ghaists on the wind, ghaists makkin daw's prayer,
ghaists himin a wairnin fer the dillin flesh, ghaists forfochten wi watter
n bluid, retourin deein fae watter n bluid, n drrrreeeeaaaams o laund
bluim i the hime, n sails unfauld i the hime, himin at the lip o the
gloamin, dowin wi the days, reddin whiles A dowe, dwyne aneath the
dream-couser's huifs... n A ken noo a life prentit in deas o rock, scrievit
wi licht in yer gairden een /

*

n A
on forlane strands
A gaithered ma letters
A leuked til the tides wi hail braith
n A whettit ma tholin on the ben-heid o
leed

فتْحِ الخلجانِ ، يُعرُّونَ دمي ، صوتي ، اسمي،
تحتَ شظايا البركانْ.

*

أتمنطقُ باليأسِ
أقودُ قطيعَ
الرغباتِ
إلى
النهرِ
فينتحرُ الماءُ
بصوتي ، أزرعُ
ورداً في تيهِ الماءِ ..
وتيهِ الخلجانْ.

*

مُرتَّهنٌ بالغِبْطَةِ ، أشْربُ ماءً دَنِساً ، وأسوِّي خِصْلَةَ شَعرِ التاريخِ ، ليبدوَ أكْثَرَ إشْراقاً في الموتِ،
وأبقى مُسْتَتِراً في العمرِ / أُشَذِبُ عُمْرَ الوجعِ ، وأجْعَلهُ رَهْناً لِمُبايَعَةِ الروحِ ، وأكْتُبُ إعْلاناتِ
الفقرِ ، وأنْحَتُ معنى الأيامْ .
مُرتَّهنٌ بالغِبْطَةِ ، يَفْرُدُني ماءُ الفجرِ ، ويَعْصُرُني الليلُ ، وأنْشَفُ قَبْلَ جفافِ الصيْفِ على كُمِّ
الليِّلِ / يتسرَّرُ في الويْلْ / يَقْرَأُ فاتِحَتي / يكبرُ في طُهْرِ مساماتي / يَلْبَسُني كالشعرِ / يُرَقِّقُ عافيتي
كالعِشْقِ / يُقَرِّبُها مِنّي / وتغيبُ / وأعرفُ أنّي لن ألقاها ثانيةً / وأغيبُ .

*

غريبٌ عن العشِّ /
صارَ لقلبي جناحانِ /
والأفقُ يعلو .. ويعلو .. فتخفقُ في قامتي وردتانِ /
على شفةِ الزعفرانِ /
سماءٌ لعرشِ القصيدةِ /
سيدةٌ عذبةٌ في تآخي الجنونِ ..
وعفَّةِ ناي الزمانِ /
وأغنيةٌ برَعَمتْ سيدَ الريحِ /
والطيرُ يأسرهُ الطيرانْ.
يا قلادة موتاي / يشربني البعدُ / أجثو كما عفّةِ البرقِ / يتسعُ العمرُ للساخطينَ وللعاشقينَ .

A set wanhoup asteep
tak me tae tinsel tae a dyst
in ma breest / the meenisters' airt is
rivin voes, thay tird ma bluid, ma vyce, ma name
aneath volcano rain.

*

A set wanhoup asteep
A wyse ma hirsel
o lists
til
the watter
whit spills hitsel
wi ma vycc A scaiter
answers tae the pride o the watter...
the pride o the voes.

*

thristin fer seil, A waucht o the gutter, n A pleat the past's hair, sae's hit
mey lowe in deith, n A loss masel i the tides / A speld hail pyne as a
hecht tae the saul, n A write declarations o puirtith, n A mak meanin
fae the draigs o the tide.

　　thristin fer seil, daw's scoors wale me, n nicht wrings me, n A'm
haisert afore the simmer drocht ower the sleeves o nicht / whit haps
me in dule / reads ma last rites / appens ma pores / weirs me like hair /
tends ma weal as a passion wad / brings near ma passion / n ma weal's
dowin / n A ken A wilna cry hit again / n A'm dowin.

*

oot the nest /
ma hairt growed weengs /
the easin rises... n rises... n twa flouers wilt in ma shaidae /
on the lip o a crocus /

في القناديلِ متسعٌ للضياءِ / أرمي رؤايَ على ظلمةٍ للكهوفِ / تئنُّ الصخورُ / ويجأرُ في دمعِها ماردٌ / ليس ضعفي الذي يتهدَّلُ في الريح / ليسَ أنا المستباحُ الجريح .
نادلني الأفقُ / كان الندى في لهاثي يبوحُ /
وقلبي يفرُّ من الخفقانِ .. ولا يستريح.

*

كتبوكَ في مَجْدِ المطر
وعلى الأثَر /
قد كبَّلوكَ بألفِ سيفٍ /
شرَّحوكَ .. وشرَّعوكَ إلى المدى / لم تنتحر !!
رسموكَ في شجرِ الخرائط / علَّقوكَ إلى المدى جوعاً ونفطاً أو بضاعةَ فاسدة.
سمكٌ يشعُّ بلونِ أطفالٍ عُراة ..
أينَ النجاة ؟!
عبأوكَ .. تقاسموكَ .. وورَّعوكَ .. ولم تجدْ وطناً بغيرِ طغاة
يا بحرُ .. يا ندمَ الجفافِ .. وعفَّة المأوى / على قيضِ الليالي ..

*

صدَّقوكَ .. وكذَّبوا المَنْفى وناموا / مثل أسرى في حدائقَ لا تُحبُّ الزائرينَ
صدَّقوكَ .. ومجدوا غَدَهُمْ / فباركَهُم بلاءٌ للبطالةِ في كهوفِ العمرِ ..
أرْجَعَهُم لماضيهمِ يؤوِّل / بينَ الحقائبِ والدموعِ. عَباءَةُ
السلطانِ تَّسِعُ الجداريّاتِ .. نارَ الشعرِ والتقوى
على رجفِ البلاءِ / تَسعُ الأراملَ والثواكِلَ
.. واليتامى /

*

سمَّيْتُهَا .. وأبحْتُ روحي للعذابِ .
سمَّيْتُها .. وأبحْتُ للتاريخ أسئلتي /
فاستلَّني يومي وآخاني الجدارُ على الحرابِ /
سمَّيْتُها / ورفعتُ زنْدي
عن جبالِ النرجسِ المغتالِ في لغتي /
وأرَّخْتُ المدارَ على جِرارِ الحزنِ .. /
لم أجد الجوابَ!
سمَّيْتُها .. فارْتَجَّ ريحُ الغيْبِ /

the lift fer a throne fer a poem /
a caller quean amang reid-wuid breither...
grace o the lilt o the tides /
    n sang blaws vieve intae the laird o the wind /
    and flicht thirls the birds.

        aw ma mortal chairm / this faurness gaups me / A kneel wi
fire-flaucht grace / the tide hauds black-nebs n luvers.
*

wi a lantren great eneuch fer ma licht / A cast ma leamin intae the
daurksome gloup / the craigs cruin / an etin pits up a greetin fleetchin
wird / hit's no ma waikness showdin i the wind / hit's no masel the
woundit n spulyit /
    claucht by the ruit o the lift / kythed wi a weet gouch /
    ma hairt shaks lowse... n disna lin.
*

thay scrievit ye wi ferlie rain
n efter /
thay cruivit ye wi a thoosan blades /
thay tirdit ye... n even on thay torturt ye / ye didna spill yer ainsel!
    thay drew a forest o chairts / thay hung ye oot tae gizzen n daise.
    fish pinkin like new skin...
    whaur's salvation!
    thay draftit ye... hackit ye... daled ye aboot... n ye cadna airt oot a
hamelaund free o thirldom
    aw faem... aw drocht o dule... n grace o a bield / tae bruik the life
this nichts...
*

thay trowed ye... but telt whids aboot exile n dovert / like captives in
gairdens unveesited
thay trowed ye... but heezit thair morras / sae they gied a malison o

قُبَّةٌ

صخرةٍ مالتْ

ونادتْ ، فاستحالَ الدربُ ماءً،

*

اللهُ .. يا اللهُ كمْ أنتَ محترفُ اليفاعةِ في المصيرِ ؟! وكمْ تمجِّدُ آيةً فيها حياةُ الأولينَ /

وكمْ أرى وجعاً كَكَسْرِ جنازتينِ / على نواحِ رهافةِ القديسِ /

مِ .. سِ .. لِ .. مِ

وِ... مِ ...سِ .. يـ ...حِ ... ي

و .. يِ .. هـ ..وِ... دِ ... يِ ..

أنا رقَّةُ الأشياءِ في المعنى / ومعنى الانقسامِ على برائنِ النباتِ / وفُجْعَةِ الصبحِ الطهورِ /

ومأتمُ الحمَّى على تعبِ الوصولِ.

sweirtie in co's o the tide
set back tae thair springheid / amang kists n teirs.
   robs o pouster mak waws... luntin poetry n haliness
   the malison chalю / houdin relicts n murners
      ... n orphants /
*

A cried her... n appent ma speerit tae nitherin.
A cried her... n appent ma speirin tae history /
A wis unsheathit by ma tide n gart til the wappen-waw /
A cried her / n heftit ma airm
   wi wirds like stocks o collit lillies /
A wis ruggit fae ma orbit by dule... /
A fund nae answer!
A cried her... n the wind dirlt wi tinsel
   a dome
       o rock dinnelt
            n greetit, n the paith wis watter
*

God... aw God hou weel d'ye ken roosie n bent set youth! n hou ye
glorifee sermons on the ancients / n hou A see pyne as a rentin o buiryins
/ n hou haliness is shilpit /
   m...s...l...m
   chr...s...t...n
   j...w...sh
A'm the lythness o meaninfu things / n the meanin o the gaps atween
thorns / the lust fer the mornin's purifeen / hame-gaun wi forfochten
fiver

Harry Giles

طاهــر ريــاض

تلويحـات

(١)

في ذكرى ما يَنسى في الحَلَبِة
رقصُ الدرويشْ
في ذكرى رملٍ يحبَّلُ بالبحرِ
فيأخُذُه عسسُ الشُّطآنِ
إلى غُرفِ التفتيشْ
في ذكرايَ
أصادفني أتسكَّعُ فوقَ رصيفٍ منسيٌّ
من مُدُنٍ منسيّاتٍ
رأسي في كَفّي قنّينةُ خمرٍ
وهواءٌ كالطائرِ
يهوي في رئتي منتوفَ الريشْ.

(٢)

يومَ تبدو السماءُ أطرى من العِهنِ
وغيماتُها أحرَّ وجيبا
يومَ يغدو الَّذي مضى طيَّ كأسٍ
طيَّ مقهىً ، ووحدَكَ المشروبا
يومَ ، أعني ، تَراكَ تهذي
بأسماءٍ من استنكفوا
حبيباً حبيبا
وترى اللهَ سائلاً عنكَ حيناً
وترى اللهَ سائلاً ومجيبا.

Taher Riyadh
Bridge translations by Luke Barrington

Waves

I
In memory
of what he forgets
in the ring
the dervish
dances

In memory
of the sand
that ropes the sea
the border patrol
inspects

In memory of me
I happen upon myself
floating above a forgotten pavement
in a forgotten city

My head is a bottle of wine
vintage in my hand
and air falls like
a featherless bird
in my lungs

(٣)

يأتي بكَ المطرُ
يا بَرَدُ،
لا حطَبٌ لديَّ ولا نبيذٌ
لا امرأة
لا شيءَ يصلحُ أن يكونَ مِظلَّةً أوِ مدفأة
يا بَرَدُ .. أعتذرُ.

(٤)

نَدماني الليلةَ كُرسي
يَشغَلُه كالعادةِ ظلّان
ظلّي وأنا أحضنُ كأسي
والآخَرُ ظلُّ الكرسي.

II

One day the sky is wool-soft
with hot clouds
when the past is folded in a glass
in a cafe
and you are the only drinker

One day, I mean, it boils and steams
in the names of those who left
one after another

and you see God, asking about you
and you see God, asking and answering

III

The rain, coldness, brings you
no firewood, wine, or lover
nothing to comfort, shelter or warm
coldness, I am sorry

IV

My friends tonight are
a chair and
two shadows

My shadow
as I huddle round my cup
and the shadow
of the chair

Ellen McAteer

محمد حلمي الـريـشـة

الكمـائـن

الطُّرُقُ المَجروحَةُ، في طَريقي، رَطِبَةُ الطَّمْي،
[بَيضَاءُ من لَبَنٍ أحيَاناً]
تَتَصَاعَدُ مِثلَ سُلَّمٍ جَبَليٍّ،
بَل هيَ هكذَا ؛ جبَالٌ أَسِيرَةٌ،
مَفروشَةٌ بِلَحمِ النَّباتَاتِ الغَريبَةِ
أخشَى عَلَيهَا خُطَايَ البَطِيئَةَ أَنْ يَذهَبَ الرَّبيعُ سَريعَ الخُطَى
في الحِصَارِ!
*

- كَمِ السَّاعَةُ الآنَ أَيُّهَا الظَّلُّ الضَّيِّقُ؟
- هل خُطوَتي تَصِلُ الأَبَدِيَّةَ ؟ أَم أَنَّهَا جَاذِبِيَّةُ خَشَبٍ
مُغروزٍ إِلَى رُكبَتَيَّ؟
*

الكَمائِنُ مَزهُوَّةٌ بِالأَمَانِ المُمَعدَنِ
والرِّيَاحُ لَواقِحُ لِلخَلفِ،
لِوَقْفَةِ الانتِظَارِ المُفَاجِئِ بِنِعَالٍ شَائِكَةٍ ..
أُكَاشِفُ سَمائي خِلسَةً وَرَغبَةً جَامِحَة:
إلهي الَّذي لا إله سِوَاه
حَدَائِقي في بَاطِنِ الإثمِ كَأنَّه مَعِدَةٌ طَاحِنَةٌ
والبُذُورُ التَتَ
سَا
قَطُ
لَيسَتْ تَجِفُّ من عَرَقِ الرُّعَاةِ وبَولِ الجُنُودِ ..
هَبني قُوَّةَ حَلِيبِ الزَّهرَةِ
وغِنَاءً مُضَاعَفاً في تُرَابِ الحَصَى

Muhammad Hilmi Al-Reesha
Bridge translations by Luke Barrington

An excerpt from The Ambushes

The routes, wounded underfoot, the moisture of their silt
[sometimes bleached milky white],
seem to rise up and above like mountainous steps.
But the mountains are captive,
furnished with the flesh of strange plants.
I am ashamed of my slow footsteps—Spring will pass away, fleet of foot,
under the siege!
*

"O Narrow shadow, what time is it now?"
"Has my gait become eternal? Or does it pull with the magnetism
of wood, pierced at my knee?"
*

Bear traps are boastful of this deadlocked peace
and the winds carry pollen to other lands.
At the sudden waiting place, thorns piercing the soles of my feet,
I reveal myself to heaven, furtively and with defiant desire:
My God, that there is no other God but
my garden in the hidden side of sin, like a stomach churning,
like pips faaa

llll

ing

وصَداً مُبَارَكاً كَي يُبصِرَ الآمِنُونَ كَلامي!

*

عَلَى عَتَبَاتِ التِّلالِ المُتَشَاهِقَةِ كَنسْرٍ مُخَضْرَمٍ
يَنطَرِحُ الخِصْبُ بِجَلَبَةٍ ضَعِيفَةٍ،
وَشَاسِعٌ دَمْنَا مِثلَ أَبَارِيقِ
غَيْمٍ
بالسَّوَاد ..
أَيُّها القَادِمُونَ داخلَ «حِصَانِ طُروَادةٍ» آخَرَ:
لِي مَا مَلَكَتْ يَمِيني مِنَ الرَّائِحَةِ الخَضرَاءِ لأَعْنَاقِ القَصَب
ولي مَا مَلَكَتْ يَسَارِي مِنْ نَدَى الملح
ومَا كانَ لي مِنَ اندِفَاقِ المَدَى!

*

بانتِظَارِي امرَأَةٌ تُرَبِّي أَزهَارَ الكَسَّتناءِ بِأَهدَابِهَا
تُخَبِّئُ شَمْعَ اليَاقُوتِ إِلَى حِصَارٍ لا يَنَدَمِل
وَعَن شُرفَةِ الرُّوحِ المُنحَازَةِ للضِّيقِ
تُطفِئُ غُبَارَ الزُّجَاجِ بِدَمعَةِ أَلَمٍ ، وأُخرَى
لِلَّمِّ يَتَعَالَقُ مِثلَ حُنجَرَةٍ لِبلادِيَّةٍ في غِنَاء!

*

[مَاذَا يَفعَلُ الجُنديُّ مُختَبِئاً خَلَفَ يَأْسِه
ومُشتَبِهاً بِظِلِّه :
يَنسَلُّ كالنَّملِ مِن آيَةِ الفُجَاءة !]

*

أَمَامَ أَمَامِي مُنزَلَقٌ للشَّرايِين:
حِينَ أَنتَخِبُ اسمِي
وَحِينَ أَتَصَدَّقُ بِزَفِيرِ لُهَاثِي عَلَى
سطوَةِ الأَعْشَابِ
في صُفرَةٍ حُلَّتِهَا
وجَفَافِ ذَهَبِها؛
يَ تَ قَ صَّ فُ

This will not dry out along with the sweat of shepherds or the piss of
soldiers...
Grant me the strength of blossom milk,
songs breeding in the dust of gravel,
and blessed rust, so that the believers may see my words!
*

Fertility is flung at the doorstep of towering hills,
like the maven vulture. It lands with a soft clamour,
and our blood swells, like pitchers
of black
cloud…

To the generations who are yet to come, inside another Trojan horse:
You are what my right side owned of the green smell of fresh-cut wheat
and what my left side owned of the water that gushed out of the salt
and what I took from time as its dams broke!
*

Waiting for me, a woman devotedly breeds chestnut blossoms
and conceals the waxen ruby of a siege that will not heal over.
Pacing on the balcony of the spirit, head bent with the weight of
oppression
she quenches the glass dust with a tear of pain, and another
in the hope it clings like an ivy throat climbing a song!
*

[What is the soldier doing, hiding behind his despair,
suspicious of his own shadow,
retreating, like surprised ants, from the plate?]
*

Ahead of my ahead, sliding into arteries

تَحتَ

تَعَبي!

*

أُحِسُّ بِمَسَافَاتٍ شَاهِدَةً عَلَى سَاعَاتي المُتَأخِّرة

أستَمِعُ للعَابِرِ يقُربي

وهوَ يَجِزُّ خُطواتِهِ بِتَجَمُّدِ إيقَاعِ مَسلَكِنَا الوَحيد

يقُولُ ، وَقَد لا يَعنِيه :

- غَائِبٌ أنَا رَغمَ غَايَاتي الخَفيفَة

غَائِبٌ أكبَرُ مِن حِصَّتي في كِتَابِ السَّمَاء ..

وأنَا ، مُستَمرّاً بِسَاقَينِ سَهميَّتَينِ ،

أخلعُ عَنهُ صُوفَ صَوتِهِ وأُجَاذِبُ حُلمي؛

ذلِكَ أنَّ دَمي لَم يَزَلْ قَابِلاً للحَياةِ بَعد!

*

[الجُنُودُ اعتَلَوا سَروَ التَّذَاؤبِ،

لا لِشَيءٍ

سِوَى قَنَاعَةِ النَّفسِ بِشَجَاعَةِ الأَسلِحَة!]

as I choose my name
and I give myself up, panting, for
the rising up of grass
its yellowed vestments—
the golden drought
B – R – E – A – K – S
beneath
my fatigue!
*

Feeling through my skin, I am witness to my clotted hours.
I keep an eye out for circumstance
—it clips off footsteps, turning the rhythm of our narrow path
to stone.
I say, perhaps meaning it:
"I am absent, despite my trivial intent,
absent and bigger than my lot in the book of heaven,"
and, advancing on my two stalky legs,
I remove myself from
its woollen voice, and contend with my dream.
So that my blood will continue to greet life!
*

[The soldiers held on to the dignity of pretending to be wolves
for nothing
but the self-conviction that comes with holding a gun!]

Juana Adcock

مايا أبو الحيات

أطفال

كلما خرجت يد طفل من أسفل عمارة
أتفقد أيدي أطفالي الثلاث
أعد أصابع أيديهم وأرجلهم
أتفقد عدد الاسنان والشعر في كل حاجب

كلما سكت صوت طفل في مخيم اليرموك
أرفع صوت التلفاز والإذاعات والأغنيات
أقرص أطفالي الثلاثة من أجنابهم
ليكون بكاء ويكون صخب

كلما جاع لي قلب
على حاجز قلنديا
أفتح فمي وأبدأ بالأكل
أكلا عاطفيا بملوحة زائدة
يسد رمق العيون التي تبكي في كل مكان

Maya Abu Al-Hayyat
Bridge translations by Danielle Linehan Kiedaisch

Children

Whenever I see an image of a child's hand
sticking out of the rubble of a collapsed building
I check the hands of my three children
I count the fingers of their hands, the toes on their feet,
I check the numbers of teeth in their mouths, every
last hair in each finely-marked wee eyebrow

Whenever a child goes silent in Al Yarmuk Camp
I turn up the volume on the TV, the songs on the radio,
I pinch my three children
to make them cry and squirm with life

Whenever my sore heart gets hungry
at Qalandia checkpoint
I comfort-eat, I
emotionally over-eat, craving excessive salt
as if I could then somehow say: enough, block out
the salt spark of the tears everyone around me is crying.

Liz Lochhead

Maya Abu Al-Hayyat

Bairns

Whinivver a bairn's haand pokes fae a run waa
I check da haands o mi ain tree bairns
I coont da fingers o der haands, der taes
I check foo mony teeth an dat der broos still hae hair

Whinivver bairns' voices whet in Camp Al Yarmuk
I turn up da soond apö da tv an wireless an sangs
I birze an nip mi ain tree bairns apö der sides
sae I can hear dem greet an warsel

Ta hadd mi haert
at Qalandia checkpoint
I oppen mi mouth an stuff mi face,
glunsh da maet o mi feelins smored in saat
ta hoid aa da stingin een dat gowl

Christine De Luca

Children

Whenever a child's hand comes out of a collapsed building
I check the hands of my three children
I count the digits of their hands and feet
I check the number of teeth
and the hairs of their eyebrows

Whenever a child's voice goes silent in Camp Al Yarmuk
I turn up the volume on the TV
and the songs on the radio
I pinch my three children on their sides
to keep them moving and feel they're alive

Whenever a heart is devoured by fear
on Qalandia checkpoint
I open my mouth and start to eat
Comfort myself with salty treats
Block out the sparks of the eyes that cry everywhere

Graham Fulton

Maya Abu Al-Hayyat

الابتسامات

للابتسامات استعمالات كثيرة:
منها مثلا ما توزعه على الفقراء والمحتاجين/
لإخفاء العجز
ترسلها برأس محني وخطوات سريعة
تدخل المقهى
ويلحقك البرد

منها ما تختصر به المسافة
بين أطفال الغرباء
الذين يشتمون كثيرا
ويعبثون بقصص أمهاتهم
الكثيرة جدا
ترسل لهم ابتسامة تفاهم
للتوقُّف عن السمع
ومراقبة الحشرات الطائرة

منها ما يكثر في الشدائد
خجولة وحائرة
تتساقط في حمامات بيوت العزاء
وفي فناجين القهوة والنمائم المتبادلة
ابتسامات تفسر الموت إيّاً كان
تلك ابتسامات فلسفية
وتحمي من السقوط

منها ما يتضاعف في حضرة الحب
ابتسامات فاضحة تتكاثر هكذا ......
يفهمها الجميع ويدّعون عكس ذلك

Smiles

There are many ways
to smile

We bestow smiles on the poor
to conceal the deficit
You smile with head bent and quick steps
as you enter the café
to hide from the cold

Some smiles shorten the distance
between the children of strangers
who swear a lot
twisting the stories of their mothers
You send knowing smiles
to let them think you understand
then tell them to forget all the noise
and watch the flying insects instead

Some of them come in times of hardship
Shy and confused
And drip in the bathrooms of mourning houses
and in coffee cups and rumours
Smiles explain death regardless
Those philosophical smiles
that protect from the fall
Smiles double in the presence of love
while obscene smiles multiply

ابتسامات ناعمة مشدودة الشفاه والعضلات والعيون
وتبعث على الابتسام

هناك أيضا
ابتسامات كئيبة
تجمعها في منديل
وتلقيها في أقرب سلة
وتحزن
تحزن جدا
دون أيّة ابتسامة فالتة

Understood by everyone
and claiming the opposite
Soft smiles tight lips and muscles and eyes
and so many reasons to smile

There are also gloomy smiles
collected in a tissue
and thrown into the nearest basket
And you get sad
very sad
without any smile at all

Graham Fulton

Maya Abu Al-Hayyat

Smiles

Der mony a ös for a smile:
maybe laid apö da pör aamos
hoidin der pörta
your head doon, pinnin alang
You set you i da café
an da cowld smoots in ahint you

An maybe dey bring closser tagidder
uncan bairns
mooths foo o swearie-wirds
nyiggin at whit der mams is telt dem
Der owre mony tales
Your smile says I ken whit you're sayin
but white yon löin
an jöst watch da flechs rise

Some smiles boarn oot o dree
blate an muddlt
dey faa whaar you're murnin, wöshin your grief
an inta coffee cups, inta gossipy sheeksin
Smiles, a shorthaand ta explain daeth
Yun farawaa smiles
dat hadd you tagidder, uphowld

An whaar love is, der poo'er is dooblt
Vyld, coorse smiles multiply an aa....
aaboady reads dem, but pits on dey dunna

Saaft smiles birsed lips an muscles an een
An whit maks wis smile

Der dimaloorie kinda smiles
an aa
Gadder dem athin a tissue
an bal dem i da nearest bin
An you turn sad
foo o döl
whan der nae smile

Christine De Luca

في رثاء شهوة الأمهات

سأتذكر وأنا أرتب سريري

وسرير طفلين آخرين

وأنا أمسح قيء أحدهما عن الارض

وأنا أفتح نافذة على غبار الشارع

وأنا أقلع شوكا من أصيص لا يخرج الورد

وأنا أقرأ وصفة لطريقة عمل المنسف على أصوله

وأنا أرتق شلحة بيضاء ثقبتها الاصابع الصغيرة

وأنا أعد ميزانية فصل الشتاء

وأنا أتفقد رائحة لحاف تفوح بالنشادر

وأنا أقلب قنوات الاطفال الستة لأجد توم أند جيري تحت الطلب

وأنا أبحث في حقيبتي _السوبر ماركت_ عن فوطة منسية

سأتذكر

وأنا أغسل جسدا بحجم الكف

وأنا أزيل بقايا خضراء من أنوف طرية

وأنا أجاهد لإزالة التشابك في شعر غزته الشكولاتة والمصاص ومربى المشمش

وأنا أقرأ قصصا عن النمل النشيط والأسود الكسولة والفقمات المهاجرة

وأنا أنزع العلكة من أسفل حذائي وقلبي

وأنا أبحث عن الطريقة الأفضل لإزالة بقع الزيت

وأنا أقضم الاظافر العشرين بعد بحث طويل عن المقص

سأتذكر

حين يلمسني طفل بالخطأ في أماكن لا تعمل

حين ترشقني الحنفية بمياهها

حين تعلنني المسلسلات التركية مشاهدتها المخلصة

حين تقرصني كفان تجتمعان أسفل الطاولة في المطعم

حين أنقب في قصص الأصدقاء عن شهوات حية

سأذكرهم كلهم

أمهات بعيون صفراء

Lament for the Mothers' Loss of Desire

            I will remember
while I am making my bed
            and smoothing the other two beds, the beds of my children
while I clean up the sick of one of them,
while I open a window onto the dusty street
while I'm paring off the thorns from that pot that does not grow roses
while I peruse the recipe for how to make real, traditional mansaf
while I mend some wee white item of underwear torn by little fingers
while I prepare a budget for winter
while I have an educated sniff at the quilt with the smell of ammonia
            and surf through all six children's channels in pursuit of
            Tom and Jerry and I search in, ah yes, the supermarket
            bag for a neglected nappy
            I will remember
While, with my soapy palms, I wash a small body
while I winkle green snot from tiny, tender noses
while I try to remove a tuggy bit, a tangle, from hair all fankled up with
            chocolate, lollipops and apricot jam
while I read aloud stories about the active ants and lazy lions and
            migratory seals
while I scrape off chewing gum from the bottom of my shoes and my
heart
while I look up the best way to remove oil stains
while I give up and bite my twenty nails after a long search for scissors
            I will remember
when, by mistake, a baby touches me there, in that neglected place
when water from the tap splashes me

كلهم مرة واحدة يندلقون أمامي
الأفخاذ البيضاء المستبيحة لساحة البيت
الغضب العابر في أوقات محددة من الشهر
القلق المفرط على فاتورة الهاتف
وجع البطن لانتفاخات لا تنتهي
تفسير أحلام الشياطين العابثة
فناجين القهوة الجاهزة للتأمل
أغنية التنورة الزرقاء فوق الركاب المفلطحة
شفاه تنز من شدة العض
ستيانات كبيرة حافظة الدنانير والقروش القليلة
مراييل منسية فوق كروش مدورة
وقصص بنات الجيران الداشرات التي لا تتوقف
أمهات بجدائل مقصوصة
وحنة طينية تسيل على الحاجبين
وشهوات ميتة

when Turkish TV series pronounce me their number one fan
when it's two wee hands that nip me underneath the table in the restaurant
when getting stuck-in to good girl-talk about a friend's life, loves and lusts
still I have to mention them
all of them –
green-eyed disapproving mothers
all of them they
come tumbling before me
with their white thighs flaunted openly only at home, only
in the domestic sphere
with their mood-swings and passing PMT anger
their over-the-top panic over the phone-bill
their constant bloatings and bellyaches
their interpretations of dreams whose
mischievous, promiscuous demons can only be
contemplated over calming cups of coffee
their singing the song of the old blue skirt
and the big fat bare knee
with their chapped and bitten bleeding lips
with spare dinars and a few piasters stuffed in their sagging bras
and still wearing the baggy aprons they've forgotten to remove over
the vast spreads of their stomachs
and their endless, endless tales
of all the errant girls of the neighbourhood.
Mothers with messy, half-braided hair
and henna mud-slides on their eyebrows
and desire
only for death.

Liz Lochhead

Maya Abu Al-Hayyat

Da passions o Midders – a elegy

A'll mind apön as A'm makkin mi ain bed
an da bed o da twa bairns
as I dicht whaar een o dem spewed apö da grund
as I oppen a window apö da stoorie street
as I brack aff tistles fae a pot dat winna growe roses
as I read da recipe to mak a richt Mansaf
as I mend whicht underwear törn bi peerie fingers
as I tink foo ta mak dö trowe winter
as I check for da niff o piss apön a twilt
an I wael trowe six bairns' channels ta fin a Tom and Jerry
an I hunse i mi bag – da supermarket een – for a hippnen I foryat

A'll mind apön
as I wösh a boady wi jöst mi löf
as I dicht green snot fae peerie saaft noses
as I varg to redd hair bizzie-wippit wi chocolate, lollipops an apricot jam
as I read stories aboot aaber mooratoogs, langsome lions an rovin selkies
as I scrape chewin gum affa da soles o mi shön an affa mi haert
as I seek foo best ta takk oot oil stains
as I bite da twinty nails whin A'm no laek ta fin a pair o shears

A'll mind apön
whan a infant happens ta touch me in a forro place
whan da tap skeetches me wi watter
whan a Turkish series wylcomes me as sincere viewer
whan twa haands trivvel me anunder da table i da café

whan spierin ithin freends' stories aboot lusts o life

A'll mention dem aa
midders wi yallow een
da hale caboodle skailed afore me
white hochs uncovered in ivery room ida hoose
tirn turns at certain times o da mont
apön a amp whan da phone bill comes
sair bellies, stentit, nivver laek ta aese
da readin o draems o mean deevils
cups o coffee ready ta steady da mind
sang o da blue skirt kirtlt abön da aesy knee
lips slaverin fae faersome bitin
slack bras stufft wi dinars and twartree piasters
foryatten peenies abön roundit bellies
a nivver-endin pört o clash aboot neebors' lasses
midders wi lang plaits
an henna slides o gutter apö der broos
an desires o daeth

Christine De Luca

في الحب

في الحب
يخسر أحد ما شيئا
الآخر
الذي سيخسر كل الاشياء
يستحق لقب العاشق

في الحب
تبدو الحقيقة
وهم جميل
أحدهم /
سيجعل من الوهم حديثا جديا
هذا تحديدا
لا يستحق لقب عاشق

في الحب
ننتصر رغم كل الخسائر
على أشياء محددة
الوقت مثلا
الملل
النوم باكرا
المستحيل
وبعض العدم

في الحب
سيسأل أحدهم

213

In love

In love
wan o dem gies up some peerie thing
Da tidder
da een dat'll loss aathin
is wirt da title o lover

In love
da truth is no unlik
a draem, a lovely draem
Een o dem
'll spaek seriously as if dat draem is real
but dat jöst
isna wirt da title o lover

In love
we win in spite o aa dat we loss
on parteeclar things
lik time
haddin oot o langer
aaber,
defyin sleep
Some o whit's missin

In love
wan 'll akse
deep questions o life
eens wi nae answer

Maya Abu Al-Hayyat

أسئلة وجودية واسعة
لن يجيبها أحد
بينما ينتظر آخر
مرور الغيمات

while da tidder waits
as da cloods pass

Christine De Luca

In Love

In love
Someone loses
A thing
The other
Who will lose everything
Deserves the title of lover

In love
Someone makes
A beautiful illusion
Appear like truth
The other
Who spoils the dream
With serious words
Does not deserve the title of lover

In love
We win in spite of all the losses
On specific things
Such as
Time
Boredom
Sleeping early
Impossibility
Some of the
Nothingness

In love
Someone will ask
The big questions
About life
No one will answer
While others just watch
The passage of the clouds

Graham Fulton

سليـم النقّـار

حصـة الرسـم

لو نستريحُ ...
ماذا سيخسرُ كوننا غيرَ التعبْ ؟
ونظرتُ حولي في الفضاء الملتبسْ
فلريما سمع النداءَ ...،
وردّ لي ؛
قلقي سلاماً
لو نستريحُ
- أأجبتني ... ؟
وصرختُ من ناري إليهِ ؛
- قد غمّس الأولاد خبزتهمْ ،
بدمعيّ وابتهالي
فهنا قلوب الناسِ ،
مثلَ الناسِ في كلّ الحقبْ
لا تبتغي حرباً .. على الأقمار والأزهارِ
- أسمعتني ؟!
قد قال لي طفلٌ يداني العاشرة :
- ها إنهم أخذوا أبي
ونظرتُ حولي ساهماً ..
- ها إنهم ... ، ...
أرأيتهم يا سيدي ؟
وتعبتُ مِنْ نظري ...،
ومنْ سفري ...،
ومنْ قلقي على الأيامِ ...،
يا أمي تعبتُ.
- هذي مباهجنا – متاعبنا
يعضُ فراشها السفرُ

Salim Al-Nafar
Bridge translation by Danielle Linehan Kiedaisch

Drawing Class

If we stopped
would the endlessness stop too?
Screaming from the fire,
I shout into darkness.
Did you hear me?
Did you answer?

The children dipped their bread in my tears
while we wrestled the chains of time
drawn to drag war onto beauty.
A child told me
'They took my father... can you see them?'
I looked, but could not see.

But I am tired
from seeing
from journeying
from anxious days
Mother, I am tired.
Delirious our joys: delirious our sorrow
And the travel nips, nips, nips, nips...

When we stop
life becomes memory.
When we sleep,

لو نستريحُ ...
، لا لمْ تَعُدْ للصحو ذاكرةٌ
ولا للنومِ أمواجٌ تؤوبُ
فرسي على الصحراءِ مصلوبٌ يُبَاحُ ...
وقبائلي؛
نطفٌ ملوّنة بريح العابرينْ
ستون عاماً أو أقلُّ ...
ولربما ستونَ من وجع
تزيدُ على الحساب ولا تضلُّ
فالوقتُ كلُّ الوقتِ مقتولٌ ...
وقاتلهُ على مهلٍ يفرُّ
لو نستريحُ ...
فهنا على كانون ليلتنا الحزينةُ
ما زالتِ الجدّاتُ تحكي؛
عن لوعةِ الماضي ...،
وأحلامٍ كسيرةْ
وتسافرُ الحسرات من قلبٍ إلى قلبٍ
لتفسّرَ الأحلامَ بالأحلامِ إذ
ضاقت بلادٌ في بلادي
وأنا الذي حفظ الحكاية ،
من منابعها على صغرٍ ،
ضاقت بي الدنيا ،
فجنَّ الشِّعرُ في رأسي ...،
ورأسيَ لا تجاقي
ستونَ عاماً أو أقلُّ ...
تمضي أمانينا إلى خلجانها
والدربُ ظلٌّ
لو نستريحُ ...
الغائبونَ الحاضرونَ
قد أودعوا سرَّ اليفاعةِ في الأغاني
وتمنطقوا غيماً ...،

our only exit is exile.
Our history is pissed into the wind:
years on years on years.
None of them lost, all of them dying.
And the murderer's footsteps lie still in the sand.

When we stop
Grandmother kindles a fire of stories,
burning our anger and dreams broken.
A breaking heart in my heart.
A narrowed country in my country.
The story
runs down in cracks from its source,
etched into my mind by old stone.
This world: the poetry lies beyond me.
I want to join the waves, but my feet stand fast.

When we stop
the present and the absent
share secrets in songs,
wrap us in clouds,
trap us in clarity,
trace the steps of the exiled in our hearts.

At drawing class
I was given
time.
On the white sheet
the child played with his shadow,
telling his smile to the open sands

لِكَي تصفو المعانِي في المعاني
من يا ترى سيرى خطاهمْ ...
في عتمةٍ وسعتْ فؤادي ؟

في حصة الرسمِ
قد كان لي؛
وقتٌ على شَرَفِ البياضِ
طفلٌ يلاعب ظلَّهُ ...
يُملي ...،
على رملِ الشواطئ شكل بسمتِه ،
وميقات الكلامِ

في حصة الرسمِ
كانت معلمتي تلوّنُ وقتنا
بخرائط الأوطانِ ،
أو بحكايةٍ عن فارسٍ؛
ركل الزمان بروحِهِ
تحكي معلمتي ...،...،
وتنطُّ أفئدة المكان من المكانِ
لكلامها صورٌ ،
وأجنحةٌ تهشُّ بشوقنا
نَحْوَ السؤالِ عن السؤالِ ،
مَنْ ضيَّعَ الأوطانَ آنستي؟
...   ...
...   ...
غَابَتْ معلمتي ،
غابَ الرسمُ والحلمُ الجميلُ
وتعبتُ من سفريْ ... وأسئلتي،
ومن وجعي الذي ...
في عمرِه طولُ
مَنْ يا ترى سيرى خطاهمِ؟

with time
to talk.

At drawing class
time is mapped onto the contours of our homeland
and on tales of knights who kick time with their souls.
Our teacher tells us the story
and colours our minds.
Putting place into heart into the question:
What happened to our teachers?

My teacher was made absent.
No drawings, no stories, no beautiful dreams.
Tired from my travel and my question
and from a life lived in pain,
I wander.
Who will see these footsteps?
Denied in love, exhausted of anger,
they stood on clouds and took
the stars from the sky and changed
the rhythm of time.

If we stop,
will time walk on?
Never thought we would lead the young into the waves.

…

What happens to us?
Are we to learn from the absent?
That wilderness does not protect life?

الغائبون ترمّلوا

وخَبَتْ مواقدهمْ ...،

لأنَّ الدربَ واقفةٌ على غيماتهمْ

خلعوا الفضاءَ ،

وغيّروا رتمَ الزمانِ

لو نستريحُ ...

ستطولُ رحلتنا على ذاتِ الطريقِ

لم نعتقدْ ؛

أنَّ الطريقَ ستنكسرْ

لنؤوب مرّاتٍ على ذاتِ الرؤى

- من أوهمَ الأولاد بالدربِ البعيدِ؟

*

سيعلّمُ الأولاد درسَ الرسمِ مَنْ؟

من سوف يعرف كم عرفنا ،

من دروسٍ قاتلةٌ ؛

أنَّ البراريَ وحدَها

لا تحرسُ المرعى ....،

فكم أعوثْ ،

وهذا للردى بابٌ

في هذه الأرضِ الصغيرةِ ،

قد كبرنا

وتكاثرت من نهرنا

مللٌ وأنسابُ

مُتَفاعِلَنْ / مُتْ ... فَاعِلُنْ

إيقاعنا ...

والطائراتُ السافراتُ

لن تستطيعَ ...

إنْ نختلفْ

فيما تفسّرهُ الحياةُ

سنظلُّ في قيثارةِ المعنى ....،

ولو نامتْ على أرضٍ سماءُ.

I battered the door of death
and found no answer.
From this small land, we grew.
From the water came our life.
Argue with this:
The skies crush our land:
our song sings on.

Lorna MacBean

زكريا محمد

الحصان

الحصان يركض بلا فارس
الشمس تلمع على عنقه وكفله
الحصان يركض على أرض العشب والحجرْ
الطيور التي شاهدته
أغمضت عيونها
الرجال الذين رأوه من على التل
جمدهم الخوف كالبرق
كلهم رأى الهاوية
إلا الحصان الذي كان يجري إليها

Zakaria Mohammed
Bridge translations by Lloyd Randle

The Horse

Riderless ran the horse,
sunshine on its flanks.
Over lush pasture and naked rock the horse ran on.
Eagles averted their gaze;
- like a lightning flash, fear
froze the men watching from the valley
 everyone seeing the chasm
the horse was galloping toward
                    except the horse...

Kathleen Jamie

مختصر أول

الشمس تلمع على عنقه وكفله
الطيور التي شاهدته أغمضت عيونها
الرجال الذين رأوه جمدهم البرق
كلهم رأى الهاوية
إلا الحصان الذي كان يجري إليها

مختصر ثان

كلهم أبصر الهاوية
إلا الحصان الذي كان يجري إليها

The Horse: a First Precis

Sunlit, its neck and back-

Birds hid their eyes.
- as though lightning-struck
              everyone was transfixed
 everyone could see the abyss
except the horse, who galloped headlong.

The Horse: a Second Precis

Everyone could see the pit
except the horse, galloping toward it.

Kathleen Jamie

السـروة

الريح فوق السطوح
لقد عبرت المضيق الجبلي وانتشرت في السهول
النار على قرونها
وخوارها يقصف الأغصان
من كسر حديد السياج؟
من أطلق القطيع المذعور؟
الكلاب المدربة لم توقفه
والخيول ارتدت مذعورة أمامه
وهو يخور ويقلب الوقت
الريح فوق السطوح
تضرب بقرنيها الأعمدة
وتسحق بأظلافها الأدمغة والقلوب
سعيد من يملك سقفاً من حديد على رأسه
فالريح لن تهدم بيته
سعيد من ربط روحه بالسروة التي لا تتزحزح
فالريح لن تهدم روحه

The Cypress Tree

This gale above the rooftops -
this gale which has swept through mountain passes
and raced down glens -

Hellish, horned wind -
bellowing and breaking branches…

Who smashed the metal stockade?
Who let loose the terrified herd?

The herd-dogs couldn't stop them,
those horses, fleeing before the wind,
whinnying and upturning time…

This storm overhead - horned wind,
battering lampposts, flagpoles, telegraph poles,
pounding with its hooves our hearts and minds -

Happy is he with an iron roof above his head
for the gale will spare his house.
Happy is he who lashes his soul to the cypress tree
that shall not be moved
for his spirit won't be broken by the winds.

Kathleen Jamie

Zakaria Mohammed

خذروف

وصلت متأخرا
بعد أن صلب المسيح
وأطلقت القنبلة النووية الأولى
وترك أحد ما خبطةً نعله فوق سطح القمر.

في الثانية عشرة والربع جئت:
الثلج على كتفي
يدي بلا كأس
ونَفَسي يجمد على شفتي.

لا أحد هنا كي أضرب كأسي بكأسه
لا مسيح كي أومن به أو أسلمه للقتلة
لا أحد كي أدبر وإياه إطلاق قذيفة نووية.

انتهى الحفل:
نثار خس وخبز
وأكؤس فارغات تماما
وأخرى بأسؤرها.

كلهم غادروا
فقط خذروف خشبي دوّرته يد آخر الذاهبين
كان يدور دوراته الأخيرة
بين فتات الخبز والخس وشظايا الكؤوس المهشمة

The Wooden Top

I got here late,
after the crucifixion,
after they dropped the first Atom Bomb
and after someone had left that foot-print on the moon

At the back of midnight, I arrived
snow on my shoulder
frozen breath on my lips

I found no one to raise a glass to
No Christ to follow or betray to his killers
No one to conspire with for a nuclear attack

The service is over
There are only empty glasses and half-eaten sandwiches

Everyone has gone
But a wooden top, moved by the hand of the last to leave, is still spinning
between breadcrumbs, lettuce, and broken cups

reeling over wine stains on the dirty tiled floor
falling between my legs

With my index finger and my thumb I pick up the top and throw it
Then I climb downstairs

Zakaria Mohammed

دار الخذروف
على بقع النبيذ على البلاط القذر
ثم ترنح وسقط بين قدميّ.
بالسبابة والإبهام أمسكت به
دوّرته ورميته
وهبطت الدرج العريض

ومبتعدا كنت أسمع الخذروف يضرب أرجل الكراسي والطاولات
...مثل ثور بقرنين داميين

As I leave, I can hear the top bouncing off the chairs and table-legs
Like a bull striking them with its bloody horns.

Salma Khalidi and Henry Bell

Zakaria Mohammed

جناح الخيبة

يدي كاسرة أطباق. تكسر كل يوم طبقا. فهي هنا تمسك بالطبق، لكن روحي تطير هناك في السماوات. أنا أكسر الأطباق كي أشرح لكم وضعي فقط. ثمة أشياء لا تشرح إلا بكسر الأطباق: أنا هنا لكن روحي هناك.

أوه، لا تصدقوا هذا. الشعر يكذب. فالحقيقة أن يدي فركوشة، ورجلي ظلعاء. لكن الشعر يقلب الأمور. يصنع جناحا للخيبة كي تطير في السماوات

أسماء

اسمي يابس وثقيل
ولذا أفتته كخبز يابس في طريقي
*

وليت لي كالأسد مئة اسم
وعلى كل اسم فروة
ولكل اسم قبيلة تسمي به أبناءها
ولا تدري قبيلة باسم الأخرى

The Plate Breaker

My hand breaks plates. Every day it breaks a plate.
My hand holds the plate down, while my soul is up in the sky.
How can I explain it?
Some things can't be explained without breaking plates.
I'm smashing them to show my dilemma; I'm here but my soul is away.

No, no, don't believe that
My hand is clumsy and my leg is lame.
Poetry flips things upside-down. It grants failure a wing and throws it into
the sky.

Salma Khalidi and Henry Bell

Names

My name is heavy
It crumbles like bread as I walk
*

I wish
I had a hundred names
and like the lion
every name had thick fur
and a tribe that would call their sons by it
and that these tribes would never know the name of the other

William Letford

Poet Biographies

Yousef Abdul-Aziz (b. Jerusalem) studied in Amman and Beirut. He is a teacher, a committee member of the journal *Awraq*, and recipient of literary awards, including the Arar Prize.

Donald Adamson is a poet, translator, and a teacher of creative writing and translation. His poem *Fause Prophets* is in a time capsule under the Scottish Poetry Library.

Juana Adcock is a Glasgow-based writer and editor working in English, Spanish and Spanglish. Her first poetry collection, *Manca*, was published in Mexico in 2014.

Abdullah Abu Bakr, based in Amman, is a member of the Jordanian Writers Association. His poetry has been published and performed across the Arab world.

Henry Bell is a writer and editor living in Glasgow. Over the last two years he has been working on cultural exchange projects between Scotland and Palestine.

DM Black is a Scottish poet, born in South Africa in 1941. *Claiming Kindred* (Arc), his first original collection for 30 years, was published in 2011.

Ron Butlin is a prize-winning novelist and is also the Edinburgh Makar. His poetry and fiction have been translated into over ten languages.

Samih Faraj is a teacher in Deheishe refugee camp, and a lecturer at Hebron and Bethlehem Universities. He has been editor-in-chief of several journals including *Voice of the Nation*.

Jim Ferguson is a poet and prose writer based in Glasgow. His collection *the art of catching a bus and other poems* is published by AK Press, and his novel *Punk Fiddle* is published by Whirlpool Press.

Graham Fulton is a poet from Paisley. His most recent major collection *Reclaimed Land: A Sixties Childhood* was published by The Grimsay Press in 2013.

Harry Giles grew up in Orkney and is based in Edinburgh. His pamphlet *Visa Wedding* was published by Stewed Rhubarb in November 2012.

Magi Gibson is an award-winning poet whose work has been widely published in anthologies and literary magazines worldwide. Her third poetry collection, *Wild Women of a Certain Age*, was published by Chapman in 2000.

Majid Abu Ghoush (b. Amwas) is a prolific poet, a member of the Secretariat of the General Union of Palestinian Writers. and a founder member of Poets Without Borders Palestine.

John Glenday is an award-winning poet. His most recent collection, *Grain*, was published by Picador in 2009.

Alasdair Gray is a Scottish novelist, play-wright, poet, painter and illustrator, best known for the novel *Lanark*. His biography was published by Cargo in 2014.

Maya Abu Al-Hayyat is a prize-winning author of novels, poetry and short stories. Born in Lebanon, she has a degree in Civil Engineering from Al-Najah University, and lives in Ramallah.

Uthman Hussein, from Rafah, is founder and editor-in-chief of the cultural magazine *Ashtar*. He has occupied many official roles in Arab and Palestinian cultural organisations.

Rania Irshaid (b. 1976) is a poet from Nazareth, where she has also worked as a journalist for the newspaper *Kull al-Arab*.

Kathleen Jamie is a poet, essayist and travel writer. She became Professor of Creative Writing at the University of Stirling in 2011.

Jackie Kay is an award-winning writer whose subtle investigation into the complexities of identity have been informed by her own life.

Tareq al-Karmy, from Tulkarm, studied at Al-Najah University in Nablus. A prolific poet, his work has been published in numerous anthologies and solo collections.

Bisan Abu Khaled (b. Damascus) is a cancer specialist in Europe. Her poetry is

much acclaimed; one of her poems formed the basis for a film about Palestinian refugees.

Henry King has completed a PhD on the poetry of C.H. Sisson. His poems have been published in *New Poetries V* (Carcanet) and a number of journals.

Mohammed Lafi is a Lecturer in English and Translation at Al-Aqsa University in Gaza, and works as a freelance translator for local and international organisations.

William Letford was the recipient of a New Writer's Award from the Scottish Book Trust and an Edwin Morgan Travel Bursary. His first collection, *Bevel*, was published by Carcanet Press in 2012.

Liz Lochhead is a poet and playwright living in Glasgow. Since 2011 she has held the post of Scots Makar.

Yousef Abu Loz's collection *Fatima goes to the fields early* received the Arab Writers Union Award. Born in Jordan, he has worked in education and culture across the Arab world.

Christine De Luca is a Shetland writer living in Edinburgh. She writes in English and Shetlandic. Her most recent collection is *North End of Eden*.

Lorna MacBean is a PhD student in Scottish Literature and General Editor of *Esharp*. She also runs a monthly arts night in Glasgow, *Fail Better*, which aims to entertain and inform, but mostly entertain.

Gillebride MacMillan works in the Celtic and Gaelic Department at Glasgow University. He is also a Gaelic translator and singer.

Aonghas MacNeacail has been a leading voice in Gaelic poetry for decades. That voice has been central to his poetry and to the new departure in Gaelic verse his work represented.

Yousef al-Mahmoud is a prominent broadcaster and poet, and former head of the Ministry of Culture in his native Jenin.

Ellen McAteer has had writing and translations published in anthologies and magazines worldwide, is a visiting tutor at the Glasgow School of Art, and has won a BBC songwriting competition.

Rachel McCrum's pamphlet, *The Glassblower Dances* (Stewed Rhubarb Press) won the 2013 Callum Macdonald Award. She also runs the Edinburgh arts cabaret *Rally and Broad*.

Samih Mohsen was born in the village of Naqoura in Nablus in 1953, and has published two collections: *Exiting the Narrow Rooms* and *Kingdoms & Peril*.

Amal el-Mohtar's first collection is called *The Honey Month*, with each piece written to the taste of a different honey.

Zakaria Mohammed was born in Nablus, studied in Baghdad and now lives in Ramallah, working in the Palestinian Ministry of Culture. He is also a journalist and creative writing teacher.

Sami Muhanna is a poet and lawyer, and President and co-founder of the Palestinian Arab Writers Union in Haifa. He is active in Palestinian political and academic affairs inside Israel.

Salim al-Nafar was born in Gaza and studied and worked as a journalist in Syria. He is author of numerous collections of poetry. He returned to Gaza in 1994.

Liz Niven has appeared at literary festivals around the world. She delivers workshops in creative writing at the Scottish Poetry Library and the National Galleries.

Tom Pow has won awards for several of his collections, most recently with *Dear Alice – Narratives of Madness* (Salt) winning the poetry category in the 2009 SMIT's Scottish Book Awards.

Faisal al-Qarqati was a prominent poet, critic, director of the Ministry of Information, and editor-in-chief of the journal Kulthoum. He passed away in 2012.

Muhammad Himli al-Reesha, from Nablus, has had works of poetry and prose translated into various European languages. He works at the Palestinian Institute for National Guidance.

Taher Riyadh has translated Elliot, Becket, Dylan Thomas and others into Arabic. He is co-director of a publishing house in Jordan, and has published a number of poetry collections.

James Robertson's novel *The Testament of Gideon Mack* was longlisted for the 2006 Booker Prize. His 2010 book, *And the Land Lay Still*, received the Saltire Society Scottish Book of the Year award.

Charlotte Runcie is a former Foyle Young Poet of the Year and winner of the Christopher Tower Poetry Prize. She has a pamphlet, *seventeen horse skeletons*, published by tall-lighthouse.

Abdel Nasser Saleh is manager of the Ministry of Culture in his native Tulkarm. A former teacher and researcher at Al-Najah University, he is author of several collections of poetry.

Omar Shabanah was born in Amman and studied at the University of Jordan. He works as a journalist and published his fourth collection of poems in 2013.

Zuhair Abu Shaib (b. Deir al-Ghusun) studied at Yarmouk University. He was a teacher and journalist in Yemen, and a book designer. He was also editor of the journal *Awraq*.

Abdel Rahim al-Sheikh from Jerusalem, teaches philosophy, history and creative writing at Bir Zeit University and the Qat-

tan Centre in Ramallah, and is the author of many literary and academic books.

Kathrine Sowerby has been widely published and awarded prizes including a New Writers Award from the Scottish Book Trust.

Murad al-Sudani is director of the House of Poetry in al-Bireh and editor-in-chief of journals *al-Shu'ira* and *Aqwas*. From Ramallah, he has worked as a journalist for several Arabic publications.

Somaya Al-Susi studied at al-Azhar University, Gaza. Now a researcher, she has authored several collections of poetry.

Ryan Van Winkle is Poet in Residence at Edinburgh City Libraries. His critically praised first collection, T*omorrow, We Will Live Here,* was published by Salt in 2010 and won the Crashaw Prize.

Acknowledgements

The editors would like to thank all the many contributors to this book as well as everyone who offered their time, support and solidarity in what often seemed like an ambitious (if not mildly insane) proposition.

In particular we would like to thank Abla Oudeh, Yasmin al-Hadithi, Buthaina Al-Awsi, Renee Ballan, Alice Guthrie, Admas Habteslasie, Oussama El-Mohtar, Rana Barakat, Mary Ann Kennedy, Reem Abu-Hwaij and Esa Aldegheri for their help and advice in several languages.

Thanks also to Kate Connelly, Mohammad al-Azraq, Olivia Crook, Roy Bailey, Alasdair Roberts, Tom Leonard, Louise Welsh, Robbie Guillory, Tony Gorman, Mercedes Villalba and Gregory Metcalfe for their support and organisational skills.

Thanks to Freight Books, The Alastair Hulett Memorial Trust, the Lord Provost's and International Office at Glasgow City Council, the Palestinian House of Poetry and The Scottish Poetry Library, as well as Dr Ghassan Abdallah, Director of CARE, Sima Ali Keishe, Murad al-Sudani, Robyn Marsack, Freya Rock, Omar Islam and Sara Shaarawi, without all of whom there would be no book at all.

Graham Fulton wishes to thank his wife Helen Nathaniel-Fulton for all of her ideas and encouragement, opinions and intuitions, and her invaluable help in solving the poetic puzzles in the early part of the process.